Catering from A to Z

Catering from A to Z

Cyrill Pogodin

© 2017 Cyrill Pogodin
All rights reserved.

ISBN: 1533247110
ISBN 13: 9781533247117
Library of Congress Control Number: 2017900424
CreateSpace Independent Publishing Platform
North Charleston, South Carolina

With special thankfulness to my wife, Lena, for all her support and love

Contents

Introduction ·xiii

Part 1   **What Is a Catering Company?** · 1

    Functions of Off-Premises Catering· 3

    How the Catering Market Is Developed· 6

    What Does the Off-Premises Catering Process Consist Of? · · · · · · · · · · · 8

Part 2   **Performance and Weaknesses of Organizational Forms** · · · · · · · · · · · · 13

    Main Processes of Catering· 15

    Structures of Catering Companies, Key Departments, and
    Distribution of Duties· 17

    Weak Spots in Catering Companies—Typical and Potential · · · · · · · · · · · 25

Part 3   **Support Documentation for Catering-Company
Activity—Why Are Service Standards Important?** · · · · · · · · · · · · · · · · · · · 29

    Documentary Support of the Sales Manager's Work · · · · · · · · · · · · · · · · 31

    Documentary Support of Events · 36

Documentary Forms for Working with Engaged Personnel · · · · · · · · · · · · · 42

Other Types of Documentation · 45

Part 4   Development of a Quality Control System · 49

Standard of Service and Standardized Control Procedures · · · · · · · · · · · · · 51

System of Control and Optimization of Functional Divisions · · · · · · · · · · · 53

Customer Feedback and Other Components of a Quality
Control System · 54

Management Evaluations · 57

Part 5   Opportunities for Promoting Catering Services and Selling Them to Corporate Customers · 59

Possible Promotional Tools · 61

The Components of a Commercial Offer to Corporate Customers · · · · · · 66

Organizing Testing Events · 69

Basic Rules and Practical Recommendations for Organizing
Testing Events · 70

How We Can Help a Customer to Review Our Work Positively · · · · · · · · · · 74

Part 6   The Requisite Equipment for Catering · 77

The Processing Equipment · 79

Equipment for Transportation of Dishes, Furniture, and Tableware · · · · · 83

The Equipment for Serving, Decorating, and Other Purposes · · · · · · · · · · · 86

Part 7	**Formats of Off-Premises Catering Events** · 89
	Various Types of Catered Events · 91
	What Determines the Choice of Format for an Event? · · · · · · · · · · · · · · · · · 93
	Space and Shape of a Banqueting Hall for Organizing Catering · · · · · · · · · 95
	The Size of a Hall Necessary for Different Formats of Service · · · · · · · · · · · 98
	Preparations before an Event and Time Requirements · · · · · · · · · · · · · · · · · 100
	"Behind the Curtains" · 101
	Space and Requirements for the Utility Room · 103
	Tents, Umbrellas, and Other Outdoor Equipment · 105
	Shapes of Tables for Servicing Different Event Formats · · · · · · · · · · · · · · · · 107
	Necessary Size of Tables and Staff Standards for Service · · · · · · · · · · · · · · · 108
Part 8	**The Menu for Festive Occasions** · 111
	Appetizers, Hot Meals, and Desserts—How to Account for Everything · 113
	Seasonal Specifics of Meal Selection and Catering · 116
	Menu Volume and Yield · 117
	How to Produce an Attractive Menu within a Given Budget · · · · · · · · · · · 118
	Beverages—Necessary Yield and Assortment · 120
	Corkage Fees · 123

The Dishware Count · 124

Glass—To Have or Not to Have? · 125

The Menu Price · 126

Calculating the Menu Price · 129

Part 9 **Methods of Organizing Hourly Personnel for Catered Events—Adhering to Corporate Standards** · 131

Specifics of Work with Hourly Personnel · 133

Working with a Personnel Database · 136

Systematic Approach to Workforce Management · 138

Multilayered Management System · 139

Providing Meal Service for the Workforce · 143

Part 10 **Specifics of Preparing and Catering for Large-Scale Events** · · · · · · · · · 147

What Is a Large-Scale Event? · 149

Preparation Schedule · 150

The Documentation Package · 152

Smoking · 155

Working Two Shifts · 156

The Space · 157

Conclusion · 159

About the Author · 161

Introduction

The catering industry has developed and evolved worldwide for some one hundred years.

The following list can all be represented by a broad term "catering": off-premises or event-related catering, provision of corporate meals (service points management in business centers, lunch arrangements in offices), ready-made meal delivery, meal provision for social facilities such as schools, universities, hospitals, military installations, and prisons, or social catering, as well as catering in transport. Event catering was one of the first to develop in the majority of markets.

There are two basic ways of starting a business. One can invest millions from the very beginning, or one can start with a small investment and grow gradually, investing profits as you earn them. A catering company can easily be started as the latter. This makes the market accessible for new players.

One of the characteristic problems in the management of event-catering companies has commonly been the lack of formalization and standardization of business processes as well as the creation of necessary documentation. This deficit makes an enterprise poorly organized and inefficient, with the result that managerial resources are solely used to solve current operational and tactical tasks. Therefore, the reactive, but not proactive, characteristic of the management of the enterprise is in effect. Hence, experience is gained only by the immediate staff but not by the organization itself. This prohibits strong development and competitiveness of such companies from a strategic perspective. That is why this book is dedicated to a consistent way of building such a business!

Catering is one of the most promising areas of the restaurant market. For companies providing off-premises catering services, it is important to have the potential to gain the market and keep the leadership. Literally everything you wanted to know about the event catering business will be dealt with in depth in this book.

PART 1

What Is a Catering Company?

Functions of Off-Premises Catering

Catering services were launched in order to provide restaurant services in places where there was either no restaurant or an equipped kitchen.

It is commonly considered that the catering industry started about a hundred years ago in the United States and that it resulted from a desire to organize the workday of a large enterprise more effectively. However, the French company Potel et Chabot, for example, mentions a reception held in 1893 for the Russian squadron based in Toulon. It should be noted that the event was not the first one organized by the company. It is not at all difficult to imagine other, similar cases that occurred long before the end of the nineteenth century. It should be noted that this premium catering firm, in Paris, was not the only one doing business for two hundred to three hundred years.

There are numerous events in the corporate world that require catering events. These include, but are not limited to, employee loyalty celebrations, media or business partners' conferences, and new product launches or other marketing objectives. Virtually any place can serve as a catering venue: an office, a country estate, a museum, an art gallery, an exhibition center, a stadium, a boat, some outdoor area on the riverside or in the forest, or just a parking lot in front of the office building. There are offbeat places like a skyscraper roof or an underground bunker that can be exciting choices also. The choice of a venue for an event is determined primarily by budget and utilizing the funds to the maximum effect. Therefore, nobody deems the lack of a kitchen a significant reason for changing a venue or a concept of the event.

However, private receptions such as weddings, anniversaries, housewarming parties, and so on. are not always meant for and organized in restaurants. These kinds of events are often celebrated in country houses, city apartments, or another rented venue.

Food provision for such events becomes a task that has to be fulfilled regardless of the availability of a professionally equipped permanent kitchen. The solution is off-premises catering conducted by banqueting departments of restaurants, hotels, and specialized companies or, in other words, by catering services.

Off-premises catering requires availability of a permanent complex that includes a kitchen and washing facilities, as well as a warehouse for equipment and kitchenware. Outsourcing to some relevant contractors may also be necessary. The whole assortment of culinary dishes is prepared at the permanent complex. The finished products and all the necessary equipment are delivered to the venue where food regeneration, table layout, and the service itself will be provided. Upon completion of the event, the equipment and table arrangements are sent back to the permanent complex, where they are cleaned and stored.

For a traditional restaurant, business catering is the most common form of diversification. As a rule, the restaurant first organizes events in its own premises and then, depending on the requests of its customers, starts practicing off-premises catering as well. The main achievement for the restaurant results in higher volume of sales. In practice, it executes one act of sale and works with one customer (corporate or private) while serving a large number of guests.

The restaurant gets an opportunity to sell a wider assortment and larger volume of extra products and services. Alcoholic and nonalcoholic beverages, rental of venues for the event, design and decoration (of tables and the event venue), organization of entertainment, lease of extra equipment and furniture, transportation for the guests to the event, and so on, all become a source of extra profit. It is especially important for small companies or for new ones that do not have a considerable volume of requests. Large companies more often than not concentrate only on their target services—provision of food and beverage—and do not engage in the related services I have mentioned.

Along with the development of the catering business, new issues arise for a restaurant. Technologies for cooking, storage, and transportation, as well as the ways of food regeneration and serving, must be utilized, which will allow for a longer expiration date compared to the standard. As a result, the restaurant is faced with different specifics: different expiration dates and cooking times, sanitary control of transport, and so on. The restaurant will need to develop its material and technical resources, including expansion in thermic, refrigerating, and washing equipment. There will be a need to either develop its own stock of tableware, service equipment, banquet furniture, table textiles, and staff uniforms or to build up business relationships with rental companies. In case of a significant increase in catering sales, an expansion in production and storage areas might be required, as well as incorporation of new staffing positions and management methods of larger numbers of operating personnel and outsourced staff.

In the restaurant market, there are companies that specialize only in off-premises catering of events. However, these are an exception rather than a rule. Such companies qualitatively develop both the service and technologies connected with provision of such a service. However, they are sometimes less stable in a competitive market. Thus, off-premises catering is often found in a company's business portfolio side by side with one or several other kinds of business activities. It might be a traditional restaurant business, ready-made food delivery (pizza, sushi, etc.), delivery of ready-made lunch boxes for corporate customers, or corporate canteen management. The latter can be organized as a food-service counter without on-the-spot, full-circle food production. Additionally, there may be cleaning services, design (e.g., floral arrangements), and events production—which may include concept development, writing of a script and a program, creating an entertainment program, casting of actors, video production, and so on.

How the Catering Market Is Developed

Quality and the level of service in each market are determined by demand and customers' requirements. Some customers may see disposable tablecloths and plastic dishes at a corporate picnic as acceptable, while others require a world-class level of service.

In small towns, catering develops at a much slower rate and scale than in big cities. The scope of operation of companies working in major markets will always be remarkably different from those with which companies work in other regions.

In New York City, London, Paris, or Moscow, events where the number of guests reaches several thousand are held quite often. Conversely, in towns where the population is less than three hundred thousand people, such a grand-scale production would be a rarity. Apart from the demand for large-scale events and the technical capability of catering companies to handle such an amount of work, one of the limitations for market development in small towns is the short list of quality venues.

Small events may be held in corporate customers' offices and, for instance, on boats in the summer. Larger events require greater space; thus, a rental of a venue is necessary, either indoors or outdoors. Options with no food can be considered as a venue for the off-premises catering. They might be various "noncore" venues such as museums, art galleries, stadiums, theaters, concert halls, circuses, pedestrian bridges, country estates, palaces, and so on. Surely in the large cities of the country there are more such venues than in small towns. Of course, this impacts market development—the majority of the regional companies point out the scarcity of the venues as one of the key limiting factors.

Catering companies always experience strong seasonal fluctuations. In some areas, 20–30 percent of the whole volume of service falls in December, when most corporate customers hold events for their employees. The next busiest season occurs during the warm season (for most of the world it's the summer months) due to open-air corporate picnic parties. February and March as well as September and October are, for the most part, filled with business events. November and January are often the "quietest" months.

There are four Ps to always consider in any product sales: product, place, price, and promotion. In order to be successful in event catering (as well as in many other services), it is necessary to consider a factor in marketing that may be called "the fifth P"—people. Keeping waiters, barmen, cooks, and kitchen workers on the staff is inefficient due to a highly seasonal nature of work. Few key cooks are, of course, on the payroll, but they work not so much as operational staff but as sous chefs, organizing the process, managing the outsourced staff, and so on. When the need arises cooks are outsourced as other operational staff. So, for example, two or three waiters and one cook will be able to serve a banquet for thirty people, and in the case of a banquet for 1,500 guests it is necessary to invite about 100 to 150 waiters and twenty to twenty-five cooks. Thus, any number of operational staff on a permanent payroll is inefficient for a company.

Event agencies are companies specializing in events organization, and their activities are not directly connected with food provision. They work exactly as agencies: outsourcing and controlling all subcontractors from venue and equipment suppliers to actors and catering service companies. They themselves become the customers of catering companies; in doing so, they contribute to the development of catering services in general. In the same way, in regional markets, these business activity and event agency markets are much more modest than in the cities.

It should be noted that there are catering operators whose work is not limited to one city only. Some embrace adjacent regions and neighboring cities, and there are those that provide catering services literally all over the world. So, for example, a New York City company can service an event in Dubai, or a London catering company can do so in Saint Petersburg.

What Does the Off-Premises Catering Process Consist Of?

The first step on the way to provision of off-premises catering service is the act of sale of the service.

In a traditional restaurant, the sales process is usually performed by a restaurant administrator. This is a person who functions as an operating manager in a restaurant hall. A potential customer comes to the restaurant and agrees with the administrator upon all the details: a menu, a pattern of services, an event scenario, extra services, and technical details. As a rule, it is referred to as reactive selling, as there is practically no proactive selling. Besides, in a traditional restaurant, the majority of events are private with a small number of guests.

In a catering company, the sales process involves not only reactive but proactive sales schemes as well. Here, the catering service company itself searches for customers. The sales process is complicated by the dilemma of venue choice and a process of approval of a number of various technical details connected to a particular venue chosen for the event. It is expected that a catering service manager, together with the customer, will make on-site visits to every potential place for the event to assess all the possibilities and make the final choice of the event venue. Unlike a traditional restaurant, the catering company often works with corporate customers, so it uses different communication channels, and there is a necessity to provide a written proposal that includes all details of the service. This proposal is usually specified, updated, and changed in the process of negotiations between the company manager and the customer. All the above is a prerequisite to the fact that in big catering companies, apart from a banquet manager (an administrator in a traditional restaurant) who deals with organization and services, a demand exists for an extra staffing position—a service sales manager.

After the sale, the information about the future event should be passed to all relevant divisions that will be involved with the realization of service: banqueting department (banquet managers), production department (kitchen), technical department (warehouse), all contractors, and so on. The information about the services ordered and specific requirements that should be taken into consideration come to the banqueting department. The order for the requested menu is passed to the production department. The technical department gets the order for preparation of necessary furniture, equipment, tableware, and textiles. In the absence of in-house transportation, an outside delivery service must be engaged. The orders for extra materials and food, as well as alcoholic and nonalcoholic beverages, are sent to the purchasing department.

There are two common approaches to organization of the internal communication in catering service companies. In the first, all information from the sales manager is passed to the banquet department, and only from there it is distributed to other divisions of the company. In the second approach, the sales manager himself or herself distributes all the information to the relevant departments; it is done in order to reduce the information loss in multiple transfers.

The banquet managers make all the necessary arrangements: outsourcing the personnel, planning the space and designing the furniture arrangement plan, developing schedules for on-site arrival and service preparation, and planning of utility space where plating, storing of utensils and equipment, and assembling and packing of the used utensils will be done. There is also the contracting of and interaction with subcontractors (connected paperwork, additional equipment rental, cakes delivery, etc.); this can be handled either by sales managers or banquet managers.

The established technology of event preparation by a manager includes the following elements:

- Drawing up an on-site event preparation plan on the day of the event
- Outsourcing work (the standard procedure of the personnel call from a freelancer database is particularly important)

- Preparation of all briefings for the staff, both initial—at the start of the event preparation—and secondary—immediately prior to the service (An individual briefing for each member of the staff on the entrusted responsibilities is also possible.)
- Drawing up a venue space plan, including the guest servicing area, a utility room, and so on.
- Drawing up a transportation plan for arrival to and departure from the site
- Drawing up a table layout plan with the full service program
- Preparation of an approval letter with all technical details for the managers of the venue
- Providing the security service of the venue with lists of the staff, equipment, and transport.

The necessary preproduction work, which includes the equipment, utensils, textiles, and so on, is prepared to be brought out to the venue. Additionally, the menu is finalized and put together. The staff is hired and given report times. Now the delivery to the venue takes place.

This delivery stage includes loading at the warehouse, actual transportation, and unloading at the venue. Loading and unloading may be performed either by a special category of workers (loaders) or by some of the waiters. It is necessary to realize that the most time-consuming tasks on-site are furniture arrangement and decoration, as well as plating of the delivered food. Thus, all the equipment necessary for these tasks must be delivered first. It should be noted that in the case of event catering, the utensils are not washed at the event venue, just as the majority of dishes are not cooked on the spot but are delivered practically cooked.

The form of cooking, storage, and serving of hot dishes also determines some aspects of preparation for the event. Hot dishes are prepared either immediately before transportation and are delivered in thermal containers (thermoboxes) or on the spot—for example, in convection steamers. Food may also be delivered cooled and warmed up in a chafing dish (this is less common). In case of thermoboxes, cooking and transportation processes of hot dishes should correlate to the service preparation process.

During off-premises catering, there is usually a banquet manager who is responsible for the process as a whole; he or she directs the work of the service staff and interacts with the customer representatives regarding all the issues concerning the service, the order of the plate service, and so on. Apart from the banquet manager, the chef arrives to the venue to supervise the work of cooks and is in charge of the plating according to the service procedure of the event. Some companies have a technical manager (a warehouse worker) present at the event; this technical manager is responsible for the organization of loading and unloading and is involved at the stage of arrival and departure. He or she is responsible for all the equipment used during the event. Thus, for the servicing of each event, a team that is headed by the banquet manager is formed of permanent staff.

Immediately after the delivery to the event venue, the furniture arrangement and its decoration and the plating in the utility room takes place. These duties are conducted simultaneously. Then the buffet or banquet tables are decorated, tables are set, bar and tea stations are set up, and beverages are served. The staff changes into uniforms, and the briefing is conducted. A minimum of ten to fifteen minutes prior to the guests' arrival, the waiters and barmen must be at their workstations.

Each employee from the operational personnel is attached to a particular area of responsibility. In case of a banqueting service, this area is represented by banquet tables. In case of a buffet reception, there should be a separate bar station and a buffet service station where clean dishes and cutlery, napkin holders, and breadbaskets, as well as all the dishes, are replenished during the event. Other waiters act as bussers and are assigned to several tables to collect used dishes or to cocktail (cafeteria) tables that are regularly cleared of the used dishes. During the service, cooks are busy with plating. In case of a buffet reception, cooks are responsible for the replenishment and replacement of the empty serving dishes. During a banquet reception, there are separate courses of cold starters, salads, hot appetizers, entrees with side dishes, and desserts.

After the service of the event has been finished and the guests have left the final collection of all dishes, packing and disassembling of the equipment, furniture, and textiles, and loading and transportation take place. Dishwashing is done in a permanent production complex.

All work described above can be presented in a diagram form as the following flowchart:

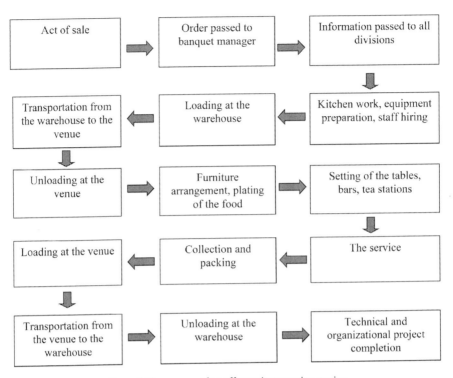

Figure 1. The process of an off-premises catering service

PART 2

Performance and Weaknesses of Organizational Forms

Main Processes of Catering

Catering implies service for every new event in a new venue, with new conditions and with new technical features. This distinct aspect of the catering industry is more complicated compared to provision of services in a permanent restaurant. Thus, this requires extra managerial and organizational effort because every event is unique.

When outsourced staff is hired, this is another factor that makes service more complicated. Outsourced personnel cannot be trained in the long run. So prior to every event, this temp staff should be informed about the company's standards. Besides, one cannot count on professionalism of the outsourced staff members since their level of training will vary. Hence, it is necessary to put emphasis on the consistency of work and service quality control. Therefore, the supervisors of standards are permanent employees working for the company—the banquet manager, the chef, and the operations manager.

Each distinct service for an event is a unique experience that can become an element of the company's competitive advantage in the market.

There are affordable possibilities for optimization of catering service operations that are often neglected. The first and the easiest methods can be the following:

- For effective work in a new venue, it is required to make a full checklist. It is necessary to take into consideration the time that guests will spend at the venue, the amount of time provided by the venue for the preparatory work, and assembling and moving the equipment after the event, as well as peculiarities of the utility room, garbage disposal, the use of an open fire, available electric capacity, and so on. This checklist can be made an official template

- for cooperation with venues. It is quite a convenient tool for managing the service process.
- When working with the outsourced staff, the following approaches can be recommended:
  1. If possible, maintain the company's own database of part-time personnel with a rating system. There should be a standardization of new staff inclusion to the database and the procedure of the personnel work invitation.
  2. When a catering company works with an outstaffing agency, it becomes the agency's task to ensure that freelancers' professional levels are good.
  3. Regardless of the method used to procure freelance workers, a development of a brief training system for the personnel at the event is essential.
  4. Develop a complex system for the management of the outsourced staff at the event by banquet managers, their assistants, and headwaiters. This requires a delegation of responsibilities: staff flow organization and its division to relatively small controllable groups during the service at the event.
- There naturally exists a lot of internal communications in the work of an off-premises catering company. This can be expedited by the use of some standardized forms for accurate information communicated between all departments. Separately, it is important to develop a system of quality maintenance, which includes compliance with the corporate work standards and additional "subjective" service quality control as well as customers' feedback. To address these issues, it will be required to form a quality control group.
- As each event involves a large amount of work, all technical details should be organized into clearly defined blocks and incorporated into the internal communication system. For example, transport working hours, accompanying information (arrival, setting, etc.), preparation schedule, space planning, and so on.

In the next chapter, we will talk about practical implementation of these recommendations.

Structures of Catering Companies, Key Departments, and Distribution of Duties

There are a variety of companies working in the off-premises catering business. They may be grouped by their characteristic organizational structure features.

The first type develops the catering business as an addition or complement to the main business area. These include both traditional restaurants diversifying their business and hotels and major restaurant holdings. The latter, as a rule, have quite a multidivisional organizational structure where one of the divisions is a catering department. Usually holding's management company is involved with finance management, human resources, business development, accounting, legal, safety, IT, and sometimes purchasing, marketing, and advertising departments. A schematic diagram is represented in figure 2.

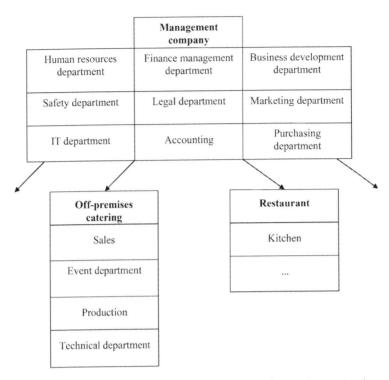

Figure 2. Multidivisional organizational structure where one of the divisions is a catering department

Within the catering division there are the following departments: sales, event management, production (kitchen), and the technical department, which includes a warehouse and transport service, decor and design, and so on.

This type of business model allows use of the same resources to work in different areas of business in the best possible way. However, it leads to duplication of managerial functions and thus cost increases and complication of immediate cooperation between the divisions.

Our second category is the organizations that can be called specialized catering companies. They may have other lines of business, but off-premises catering is their main focus. Such companies can be nominally divided into large (fig. 3) and small (fig. 4). The former, in the scale of their operations, belong to medium or large business and have formidable sales volume of their own services and the capability to serve events with a large number of guests. The latter are often small businesses and have only twenty to thirty permanent employees.

There are other differences in the organizational structures of big and small companies. For the most part, these are connected to the distribution of certain responsibilities between the departments. The major trend is the following: as a company grows, it requires greater specialization of its departments and employees. Of course, there is no ideal organizational structure of a catering service—each company is unique, and there are an infinite number of variations.

A large banqueting service can have quite a multidivisional organizational structure allowing for large volumes of requests. First of all, the marketing and advertising department enables the company to announce itself in the marketplace. Then, there is a sales department whose employees are directly responsible to work with customers and search for new customers. Additionally, there is an event department as well as purchasing, production, administrative, finance and accounting, human resources, and technical division. Sometimes a company may have its own transportation department as well as design and decoration.

More simply, the organizational structure of a large specialized catering company can be presented as follows.

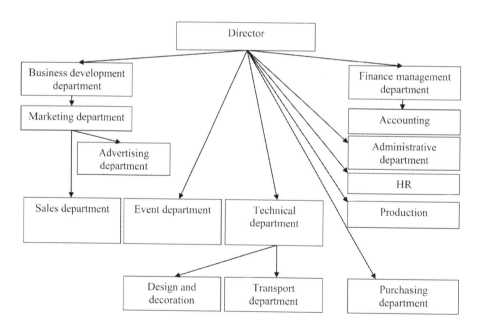

Figure 3. Organizational structure of a large specialized catering company

Sometimes a company that is entering the catering market tries to copy the organizational elements of a key industry player. This can prove dangerous. Every company has its own history of development and formation of its team, its own customer niche and scale. When a small company tries to copy the leader, this is almost always inefficient and at times lethal.

Let's review just one typical example. In large catering companies, the duties of sales and event management are usually divided between two separate departments. The sales manager works with customers until the agreement is signed and then passes the order to the event manager, who can also be called the banquet manager or service manager. In smaller companies, these duties are performed by one person—an account manager or a project manager. Combining these duties has the following benefits. First, it affords flexibility and interchangeability of managers. Second, it is convenient for the customer to have one point of contact in the company throughout the entire engagement. Third, it shortens the time it takes to transfer the information, therefore reducing the risk of losing or distorting it. Fourth, the manager is positioned to take into account the technical capabilities of the company already at the stage of selling the service and form a proposal that fits the best. Fifth, a manager who combines duties knows the service inside out, as opposed to a sales manager who is only involved in customer acquisition and sometimes doesn't participate in the actual process of catering.

The list of benefits in combining the duties of sales and event management in one person can be continued. But it also has an opposite side. A sales manager, typically, works regular hours. When the duties are combined, the manager's schedule becomes unpredictable because catering is performed at any time on any day of the week. Certainly it negatively impacts his or her ability to actively conduct sales. Besides, the job requirements for a person who combines the duties of sales and event management are much higher, making it more difficult to find suitable candidates.

All these challenges become critical in large companies as well. Practically any catering company that is actively growing sooner or later meets the necessity to separate sales and event management into independent departments.

Depending on the size of a company, there are further specifics of management.

In large companies, procurement is conducted by a separate group, perhaps even a whole department. In smaller companies, this duty is divided between the chef (head of production) and the head of the technical department (warehouse). The former is responsible for working with food vendors, and the latter works with the vendors of equipment, consumables, and beverages. Dividing these duties provides greater flexibility and precision in vendor management. The disadvantages are the lack of a systematic approach when having two separate procurement groups and two points of management control instead of one.

It is common that a smaller company may not have a distinct marketing and advertising department. Therefore, related duties are split between the CEO and the sales department. The advantages are fewer headcount, smaller payroll and other fixed costs, and a perfect understanding of the customer base. The key disadvantage is the conflict of competences. A marketing manager must necessarily possess creativity, while a sales manager is typically a pragmatic person with a systematic rational mentality who finds creativity challenging. As a result, marketing efforts in such a company can be weak and amateurish, and its advancement in the market can be hindered. Large companies can't afford this, so they create dedicated departments that are properly staffed and equipped.

Further on, smaller companies typically do not have business development managers and a corporate finance department. The corresponding duties are performed by the CEO, who decides on the direction for the company's growth and its positioning in the market, while delegating specific tasks to other personnel.

The following should simplify the organizational structure of a small, specialized catering company.

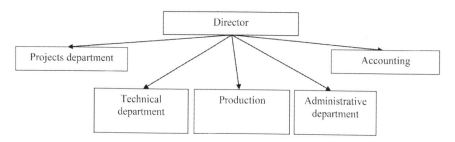

Figure 4. Organizational structure of a small specialized catering company

We should discuss the possibility—and at times the necessity—to outsource certain functions to third parties. The majority of players in the catering business outsource such functions as technical maintenance (electrical and plumbing) and sometimes cleaning of facilities. Also outsourced can be care of table textiles, design and flower arrangements, courier services, transportation, and sometimes accounting and HR records.

Warehousing in its entirety can be outsourced. A catering company can either own its entire equipment base—furniture, textiles, tableware—or rely on rental services. If so, warehousing can be limited to the company's own high-end dishware and elements of decor. In a similar fashion, there is a choice between developing a company's own database of hourly employees or using the services of an outstaffing agency that specializes in freelancers. Basically, anything that is not the primary function of a catering business can be outsourced to a third party. This allows the company to focus on its primary business.

What areas to outsource is a decision that depends on a company's structure and the specifics of its organization. For example, if one of the key offers is a daily lunch service, then the caterer is likely to have his or her own vehicles. However, if the company only caters to events once or twice a week, it might be more practical to engage a transportation vendor.

There are two practical solutions for textiles. A company must either organize its own laundry facility or outsource it to a professional laundry. Naturally, your own laundry will be more flexible, fast, and efficient in dealing with heavy stains and minimizing the volume of fabrics that have to be put out of use. An outsourced laundry service is efficient when dealing with particularly large volumes of textiles, even though flexibility will have to be sacrificed.

Much rarer is outsourcing the first stage of sales: phone marketing, also known as cold calling, aimed at establishing the initial interest in a decision maker, introducing the company, and possibly arranging for the first meeting. It can be done by specialized CRM (customer-relations management) agencies that offer services related to establishing and developing effective customer relationships from market monitoring and attracting potential customers to providing quality services and implementing customer loyalty programs for existing accounts.

Selecting a CRM vendor requires the utmost attention. The first step is to develop a detailed algorithm of potential customer communication. Each stage, including introductions, presentation of the company and its services, answering frequently asked questions, and feedback processing and such, should be described in detail. Calls will be conducted by the CRM agency's call center agents, who will be trained in the basics of catering services knowledge and in a particular company's specifics, as well as in the general techniques of selling these services.

After the initial training, test calls are conducted. CRM agents call the catering company's managers and conduct mock-up calls as if talking to potential customers. Afterward, the managers can give the CRM agency their feedback with regard to the agents following the protocols and what might needs to be handled differently. After that, the agents start calling potential customers in a contact database that, by the way, can also be provided by the CRM agency. All phone calls should be recorded so that the catering company can conduct selective quality checks and the managers can pick up a conversation with a customer where an agent left it. When talking to potential customers, agents can introduce themselves as assistant account managers, preemptively warranting their limited decision power. This practice is traditional in service sales and is tried and tested, for example, in the banking and insurance markets.

Besides the catering departments of holding companies and specialized catering companies, there are also companies in the market that can be called "catering agencies." Their permanent headcount only includes a few employees, and they have neither their own production facilities nor warehouses.

Catering agencies work according to figure 5. Upon engaging a customer and negotiating a contract, they recruit production facilities (stationary restaurants or commercial kitchens), rent the equipment, furniture, tableware, and textiles, and find hourly employees and all requisite vendors in order to organize an event. This way, even the food processing itself can be outsourced, with any fixed costs minimized. The headcount only includes account managers, who often combine the duties of sales with event management.

The key advantage of this organizational form is minimum fixed costs. The disadvantage is in the fact that every event has to be organized as a new project (starting from selecting a production facility). Another weakness is the lack of stability in high season, when rental equipment and tableware are in short supply due to heavy demand. Additionally, when a company outsources the food processing, there is little leverage to control and manage the quality of service.

There are many examples of high-end catering agencies whose main competitive advantage is not a broad base of expensive equipment or an ultramodern production facility. Their advantage lies in a perfectly organized process of catering and quality control. So catering agencies can still trump the playing field. Of course, this is open to discussion, but the fact is that it is precisely the ability to provide high-quality service that some caterers lack.

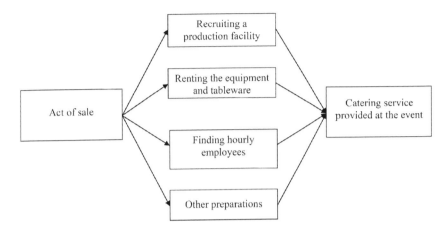

Figure 5. Catering agencies' work

The extreme form of simplifying the structure of a catering company is completely outsourcing an engagement to a competitor. Sometimes even specialized catering companies do that when selling beyond their capacities. For example, this can occur when the company schedules too many events for one day or has one event with a particularly large headcount. In the first case, it will outsource one or more of the events scheduled for a day. In the second example, it may invite a competitor to collaborate at an event. In a high season such as December, even large-scale engagements may migrate from one caterer to another.

In summary, there are multiple ways to organize a catering business. Each form has its own advantages and weaknesses that must be taken into consideration when deciding on a company structure.

Weak Spots in Catering Companies–Typical and Potential

In order for a catering company, of any organizational structure and distribution of duties, to consistently provide high quality of service, it is necessary to establish the standard workflow. This minimizes the impact of personal traits and the experience level of the personnel involved on the quality of service. The foundation is to standardize business processes and form a document package that itemizes managers' duties and provides for an exchange of information at each stage. When working on the document package, it is important to consider the weak areas of the business.

The following aspects of catering business can be considered its weaknesses.

The initial contact with a potential customer. Many companies do not standardize this process, and its outcome is completely dependent on the level of experience and professionalism and the personal qualities of a manager.

Negotiating a commercial offer. When a company originally enters the market as a stationary restaurant, it is not uncommon that its commercial offer will be limited to its current menu. Details to be discussed include the specifics of the venue, technical specifications of catering at that venue, services that are included in the menu price, and additional conditions such as serving beverages, bringing a customer's own alcohol, and decorative elements of the tables and the venue that are included in the cost or available at an additional charge. Many times, the offer frequently lacks technical specifications such as the size and shape of chairs, textile colors, time required to prepare for the event, and subsequent clean-up time. The latter is especially important when an event is planned at a customer's space, such as an office or a private house. Also, catering companies tend to neglect information about their competitive advantages in a commercial offer. Surprisingly, even reputable specialized catering companies that have been in business for over ten years, even those in the high-end segment, often display very weak efforts to present their offers to potential customers. Their offers are barely a menu with limited technical specifications and notes. This is insufficient for most events.

Active sales. An account manager's activities in selling to potential customers often are insufficiently thought through or are poorly organized. For example, the structure and content of a potential customer database can be inefficient and impractical. As a result, the process of searching and acquiring new customers is either entirely absent or impacted by the personality of the account manager. Frequently, the manager does not formally report his or her efforts and does not provide a sales forecast. Subsequently, the finance department (and CEO) does not have sufficient information to predict sales and production volumes in the present and future.

Many catering companies oversimplify the stage of event preparation, which inevitably impacts the quality of service and the frequency of issues and failures. The first weak link is the lack of standardization in record keeping. For example, in one company the pages in an order that an event manager sent to production (kitchen) were numbered, but the total page quantity was not stated. This small detail led to a situation when the lunch and the first tea break for a conference were produced correctly in desired volume; however, the second tea break was not prepared at all because it was provided on the last page, which had been lost. As a result, at the event the manager discovered that he was six hundred sandwiches short. Similar situations occur when an event management department sends instructions to the warehouse or vendors, decorators, and transportation.

Often companies do not produce a detailed event plan, and the event manager finds himself or herself in no position to predict how much work needs to be done in a given time interval and whether the personnel are adequately tasked. In *force majeure* situations, the preparation can take longer than planned, which is absolutely unacceptable when guests expect an event to start at an agreed time.

It is not uncommon that companies skip a transportation plan. Of course, the event manager, the technical manager, and the transportation manager do certain planning; specifically, they assess the time needed for loading, moving, and unloading the equipment. But they forget to inform others or, at best, inform them verbally. As a result, event plans and transportation plans can be violated.

As mentioned earlier, many catering companies attract freelance personnel, which creates its own challenges. For example, when first interviewing a candidate, not all required information is collected, nor are all the rules of conduct are communicated. Typically, this happens because there is no standardized process of including freelance personnel in the database. For another example, the waiters are not fully informed when called for work. As a result, they show up in unacceptable footwear, at the wrong time, expecting a different pay rate, or planning to finish earlier than the time expected by the event manager.

This issue is aggravated by the fact that hourly personnel cannot be trained for a long-term perspective. Therefore, providing proper instructions is paramount. Many companies lack any standardization in the process of instructing personnel, without written guidelines. This results in instructions given in a disorganized manner, and the personnel end up developing their own ideas about the rules of proper conduct.

The event manager is responsible for the guidelines and is the decision maker. He or she often doesn't have the luxury of delegating tasks to other employees. For example, when there is no written diagram of the way the tables should be set, the manager has to personally participate. The same applies when there is no furniture layout, no diagram of equipping the utility space, and so on. Of course, it is much less of a challenge when setting up a small event; it will possibly not impact the quality of service. But when serving to an event of three hundred to five hundred guests, it can cause critical issues.

When working with the catering venues, the following should be taken into account:

1. The time restrictions for preparing and conducting an event
2. Technical conditions such as the area and location of the utility space, the trash removal, and availability of electrical supply, water, and sewage
3. Availability of a changing room, cleaning services, and cloakroom attendants

All these specifics are often not negotiated in detail or not discussed at all. As a result, discrepancies in expectations of the caterer and the reality of the event space are only discovered at the day of event.

In short, missing detailed documentation that covers various specifics of the event preparation and execution stands in the way of providing timely, high-quality service.

I would separately mention that a typical weak link in catering is the absence of a quality control system. As a result, a customer that regularly enlists a particular caterer discovers that he or she can't expect a consistent level of quality and therefore does not see any sense in being loyal to a particular caterer.

In summary, analyzing typical weaknesses in workflows of catering companies is a complex and challenging job with an abundance of possible issues. Therefore, it is necessary to standardize the workflow in order to significantly reduce the human factor and focus on providing a consistently high quality of service. Standardization of the workflow should be complemented with developing a package of documents that help systematize key business processes at all stages of a production.

PART 3

Support Documentation for Catering-Company Activity—Why Are Service Standards Important?

In order to avoid problems with potentially weak links in a catering company service, one should think about how to bring the "human factor" to be an advantage instead of disadvantage. There are two possible ways to bring about a solution. The first one is constant employee training. The second is the standardization of activity, which absolutely will be a good addition to any program of staff training and development. To set a standard for a specific employee position means providing a detailed description of what to do and how to do it. However, most problems associated with the "human factor" occur at the points of different staff members' interaction and at the intersection of activity of various company structural divisions. This is precisely why the development of documentary form is extremely useful to support the company activity at large.

Documentary Support of the Sales Manager's Work

One typical weakness of a catering company seems to fall in the category of the lack of a standardized procedure for sales managers. The following is needed:

1. A prescribed method to accept a customer's initial request
2. Development of commercial quotation
3. Customer database creation
4. Standardization of customer service reports and the development of sales forecasting forms

In some companies, these functions are distributed among different staff members. Nevertheless, each of these listed processes requires its own rules of procedure.

To accept a customer's initial request, it is necessary to take into account the following components. First, the customer's contact information, including name and surname of the contact person, name of the company, landline number, mobile phone number, and e-mail address should be documented. Secondly, all request details—acceptance date, offer deadline to the customer, name of the manager who accepted the request—also should be recorded. It is necessary to document all the information on the upcoming event. What is the expected number of guests, and what is their profile (company employees or company customers, age groups, ratio of men to women, presence of children, and so on)? What the event is for? What is the proposed form of restaurant service (banquet, buffet, cocktail, etc.)? Is there a proposed venue, or does one need to be selected? What is the date and time of service?

Additionally, it is necessary to submit an estimated budget for the service or indicative budget for service per person. The customer by no means always provides such information. This occurs because he or she may be afraid to receive a proposal with overestimated prices. Often, the person initially communicating with the catering company simply does not have all the details.

It is imperative to clarify the customer's preferences as to menu composition, drinks assortment, and the list of necessary additional services. It may be useful to clarify the previous experience of events carried out with the customer company.

It is very convenient to tabulate all this data in some form, which will be helpful when the service request is accepted. To use this form of request for statistical data processing is a good practice to include in a list of advertising sources from which the customer could find out about the company's services.

When creating a customer database, it is necessary to take into account a number of nuances. Contact information should be given in the form of several separate blocks: phone, e-mail, and contact person name with indication of job position and department in which this employee works. In addition, it will be useful to understand the staff of the company and the scope of its held activities. If the companies from the database are distributed between several sales managers, it is necessary to specify the name of the manager who is responsible for each company.

The customer-relations manager's report form can look like the database table with the addition to one of three blocks: the date of last manager call, the date of scheduled follow-up call, and comments as to the results of discourse with the customer and his or her interest in services at this stage of negotiations. A manager, in real time, can fill out this form and in this case, the head of the customer service department (sales department) will be able to receive the latest information on ongoing work.

Big companies need to develop a sales forecasting form. This form can be prepared for the current month and the following one, with regular weekly updates. Each project that is currently in progress will be included in this form with indication of probability that the project will turn into a real event service. For that end, it will be required to form a so-called sale probabilities table, which will be filled out in accordance with the stages of work with customers from receipt of initial request to the date of conclusion of contract. The figures in the table may be checked and adjusted in the course of operation with a sales prediction based on actual statistical data. For preparation of a basic probability table, it is possible to project with the following figures:

> Probability level 0.1— - The request from the customer was received. In response to it, the proposal was sent.
> Probability level 0.2—Submitted proposal is for tender; the customer has not yet determined the venue.
> Probability level 0.3—The proposal is for tender; the customer has determined the event venue.
> Probability level 0.4—For tender, only two members were left. An amended proposal was sent.
> Probability level 0.5—Customer verbal confirmation was received.
> Probability level 0.6—A specified preliminary order cost sheet was sent.
> Probability level 0.7—The details were received; the documents are in the preparation stage.
> Probability level 0.8—Finished documents are in the possession of the customer for signature.
> Probability level 0.9—The documents are signed and received.
> Probability level 1.0—The event is paid.

What is "sales forecasting"? When marketing a company's services, we do not know what the volume of sales will be in the next month, and if this month will be active or "blank." This information is very important for the chief financial officer; he or she knows the expenses for each month and, of course, would like to balance them by financial returns.

For financial planning, we can start out from the customer requests that are in the works as of the date of forecast preparation. First, we determine the forecast period and, second, the frequency of sales forecast preparation.

My recommendation is to make the forecast period equal to two months. For example, during whole of April, we make forecast for April and May. In early May, we will make the first forecast for June. The frequency of sales forecast updating could be weekly. In other words, the forecast for the current and the next month will be adjusted every week—for example, every Friday before midday.

Sales managers are provided with the form, to which they add forecast data. In this form, per each project that is in process, record the date of the event, company name, and the number of attendees. By the way, the number of attendees can always be in flux.

Today, the customer company has planned the event for a hundred people; next week, when the forecast is updated, it may easily increase up to 120 or decrease to 80. Therefore, after the data on the number of people, it will be useful to input the changes in this value.

The next graph in the sales forecast should be the "minimum base budget." This is a pessimistic forecast of the minimum amount that the company will receive from the customer, on the condition that the event will take place. Sales volume according to a pessimistic scenario is needed in order to overvalue the predicted figures. Allow me to illustrate.

The customer ordered the banquet menu, and the manager offered him cost-effective and average-per-cost options. Moreover, the customer said that he would need alcoholic drinks. He was offered an entertainment program and services according to the initial information. Thus, in the form of sales forecasting, in the "minimum-base budget" section we point out the cost of the most economical menu that is multiplied by the number of persons. However, this figure doesn't include additional services (alcohol, arrangements, and so on). After this value, we should specify the details about its change in comparison with the previous week due to the menu correction. This means a value correction, which takes into account the number of event participants. After calculating the minimum-base budget and its changes from the date of preparation of the previous forecast, we should specify the probability value at which the event will take place.

If we only received the initial request from a potential customer, this is the lowest degree of probability, which equals to 0.1 or 10 percent. When the event is paid, this is the maximum value of the probability, which equals 1.0 or 100 percent. The same is true in regard to the number of event attendees and the minimum-base budget. The probability of each event of each project coming to fruition will be adjusted weekly in accordance with development of the negotiations.

The last block in the table is in fact the final forecast. Actually, this is a minimum-base budget multiplied by probability value. The convenient way to arrange all specified values is in a series of columns in a single table, each line of which will describe a separate event. In addition, you must specify the name of the manager and/or supervisory person.

Each employee fills in the table by each of its events. The sales director links all the forecasts into an integral whole. This provides an overall picture and ability to estimate total predicted sales volume. In the forms' headers of sales forecasting, it is convenient to specify the month for which the forecast is made and the date of its preparation. Other information that may be included is whether a particular sale is active or passive.

If the event is transferred to the following month or canceled, all columns of forecast table should specify zeroes. This is necessary so that the sales director sees that the event was previously scheduled but was postponed or canceled. This row with zero values will appear in the forecast only once.

The forecasting figure of total sales volume for the current month will be changed every week. In addition, during the first weeks, the forecast, in terms of finances, will be rather modest and much less than the future real sales figure of current month. Closer to the end of the month, the forecasted amount will almost "merge" with the actual one. This will provide the chief financial officer a status that is close to the real value of sales volume.

When the forecast includes a big event with large budget but with a low likelihood rating of it actually happening, the head of sales may independently mark down this factor or exclude it from consideration altogether. It will not allow distortion of information on actual sales volume, due to the loss of the tender by the company. In addition, it is very important that the probability scale be built accurately to what is really happening in the process of service sales. After all, according to the proposed system of probability, only 10 percent of all requests are brought to fruition. From verbal confirmations, only half will be paid.

By the use of regularly updated forecasts, we can track the sales of the company in the same period of a year or two ago. This will allow a company or department head to analyze the data on key indicators, including the number of events that are in works, the total forecast for the week, the amount of forecasting budgets, and so on. Having the sales forecast in tabular format allows the sales director to see an overall picture and to represent the dynamics and assess the prospect of a possible sales volume. Based on this data analysis, he or she can provide the manager with recommendations on submitting to major customers of more competitive commercial quotations, special conditions, and so on. An additional point is that the sales director can evaluate the work of the department, comparing the data with the same periods of last year.

The following is a minimum set of documentary forms that should be used by the services sales manager:

1. The form of the primary customer request acceptance
2. Database form of both current and potential customers
3. Form of customer service report
4. Sales forecasting form

Documentary Support of Events

The second, equally important stage in the customer service work of a catering company is the period of immediate preparation for and service of events. For the operational manager, it is necessary to standardize, in documented form, all organizational preparation. Therefore, to set high standards, the following basic documents are necessary:

1. The menu that is ordered by the customer in the form of an application for production
2. A standardized application form for the technical department (or contractor rental company), clearly indicating all equipment, tableware, and textiles needed
3. A list of alcohol, soft drinks, and hot drinks (specifying the number of units/portions and volume) along with the previous application for the technical department
4. A transport-plan form
5. A functional list that covers the structure of the event, for the production and technical department (in addition to the applications that are addressable to these departments)
6. Detailed schedule of preparation at the on-site event
7. Plan of utility services room organization
8. Layout of tables in all areas
9. Distribution of the equipment and drinks among all venue areas, for table setting
10. Lists of equipment that will be rented from third-party contractors

11. The total list of food plating (with specification of serving dishes) and serving time of each item
12. The scheme of table setting with description and schedule of plate service
13. The list of issues to be agreed with at the rented venue, on the basis of which a "letter of agreed conditions of work at site" will be prepared
14. Personnel instruction
15. A hard list, with phone numbers, of all personnel that specifies place and time of the meeting (the database of engaged personnel or information from a hired personnel agency)
16. Lists of personnel, equipment, and transport to be provided to the administer of the site
17. File of communication with the customer at the stage of event preparation
18. Copy of the customer contract and the forms that specify other contingencies such as event prolongation (I would recommend having two copies)
19. Event scenario from the event agency (in case of event organizing agency involvement by customer)

Of course, with smaller or regular-scale events, managers will be able to use a reduced list of documents. This full complement of forms is needed for large events.

In the above-mentioned list, the main documentary forms are numbers 2, 5, 6, 13, and 15, the structure of which we will consider in detail. For the other forms (1, 4, 7, 11, 12, 14, and 18), it will be enough to only comment.

The positions under numbers 3, 8, 10, 16, 17, and 19 are quite simple, and they will not require detailed explanations.

In the header of each prepared form, summarize the event, along with the name of the responsible manager, the date, the time and venue, the name of the customer's company, the number of guests, and the service format.

The menu form should be an application for production with *all* its pages numbered and indicate the total number of pages (for example, the first page will be numbered as 1/3 where 3 is the total number of pages in the menu for this event). Each corresponding meal should have its output specified in grams/ounces, not only portions.

The standardized application form that is sent to the technical department should be prepared by the events manager. It should be in two parts: an equipment (including all tableware) application and a textile application. The structure of the two parts is identical. As with the menu pages, it is necessary to number the application, indicating the total number.

The following sections are required in this technical application: equipment names and the numerical characteristic of each unit, the number of each item that is the available at the depot of the company (from the data of depot inventory), the amount requested to be taken out for the event (to be filled up by manager when preparing the event), and, finally, the amount to be returned from the event (to be filled out upon return to the depot after the event's end).

The transportation plan includes a list of the stages of transport operation. This must include time of arrival, time of departure, and the time that is allotted to each stage. Preplan and enter time required for loading at the depot, transportation to the event venue, off-loading at the venue, and reloading after completion of the event, transportation, and unloading at the depot.

A functional sheet for the production and technical departments is prepared in addition to applications that are addressable to these departments. This should include all details concerning the service. The functional sheet form may contain the following information:

- The name of the event site and its address and details
- All contacts that are necessary for the event manager to interface with (contacts of the customer, site, and all contractors per this project)
- Format of service and event theme
- Presence of own furniture (or should it be delivered) at site
- A brief description as to where and how all the tables (buffet lines, guest seating, cocktail tables, bars, tables of used tableware, etc.) should be placed and how they are to be served
- When and where each group of hired staff is to arrive and their total number

The presence of such a document relieves the employees of the different departments of the need to clarify and coordinate many small details and provides full information about the event. If a need arises to transfer the project to another manager due to vacation, illness, or conflicting events on the same day, the probability of technical details being lost is reduced significantly.

The detailed schedule of preparation is indispensable to any extensive event. After all, at this stage of its preparation, the details are copious, and even an experienced manager will not be able to control the entire range of issues without this carefully thought-out preliminary plan. The situation is exacerbated by a great number of personnel who are subordinate to the manager. When there is a staff of more than fifteen or twenty, the manager must enter the intermediate control link in the form of supervisors or senior waiters, who will manage by smaller groups and who will be subordinate to the manager directly. Therefore, the preparation plan takes into account not only the entire list of workers but also their partitioning between personnel groups.

It is also important to plan the organization of the utility services room. This room should be organized into three functional blocks: the zone of cooks' work that serves the dishes, the zone of used crockery and cutlery collection, and a storage zone of inventory and equipment. The zone of hot drinks service (which in the case of a standing buffet will be directly in the guest service zone) will be added to the banquet format. Convenient and quick access of personnel to all these blocks should be provided. If this is impossible, it is necessary to arrange these zones so as to maximize the availability to at least the cooks' work zone and used crockery collection zone. Equipment storage and hot drinks preparation zones, in this case, may be relegated to the more remote areas of the utility room.

A general list of plating for the head cook is required. This list must indicate the type of meal and how much of it will be used for each served item. Additionally noted should be the time of their readiness. This list will relieve the head cook of the necessity to request additional information from the event manager.

For supervisors, the table-setting schematic, with descriptions and regulations for plate service, is required. The schematic, apart from cutlery, meals, and drinks, must contain such details as cloth napkins, decorative items, and so on.

The next important document that should be prepared before the start of preparations is a "letter of agreed conditions of work at site." This document contains all company agreements with the venue. It may be prepared based on the list of issues, which the manager, together with the customer, uses at the stage of site selection for event.

A basic list of issues when coordinating technical conditions with the venue may be as follows:

1. Full name and phone numbers of contact persons, including the ones who will be available to solve any problems should they arise at the event
2. What is the cost of venue rental and what is the length of its use?
3. What is the cost by the hour of the venue's rental should the event go overtime?
4. Is the engineering and utility services room included in rental payments?

5. Is the existing furniture (type and number of tables, chairs, etc.) included in the rental figure?
6. Is there availability for wardrobe service? Is this included in the rental figure?
7. What is the availability of caretakers, and what is their number? Is this included in the rental?
8. Is there a cost for dismantling?
9. What is the availability of lighting equipment and use of power? What is the cost of its use?
10. What is the availability of audio equipment and power? What is the cost of its use?
11. Is garbage removal needed after the event?
12. Is there a supply of water in the utility room?
13. Is there a supply of electricity, and what is its maximum power?
14. Is floor covering required in the utility services room?
15. Is there a lockable area to store personal belongings and change of personnel clothes? Is there a storage area for alcoholic drinks?
16. Is it necessary to submit lists before the event of personnel, equipment, transport, and so on? And what is the lead time?

These questions provide the manager with a checklist so that he or she will not miss anything when coordinating technical specifications with a venue. It will also be a basis for preparing a letter of coordination. This letter of coordination will be the document that is required for interaction with all services of the site directly on the day of the event.

Very often the customer, during the event, asks for a "continuance of the banquet." If this occurs, it is necessary to take into account that this means additional costs: waiters' payment, transport delay, and so forth. Therefore, it is paramount that all contracts stipulate the cost of each additional hour of service. Usually, such costs are 2–5 percent of the cost of the banquet service.

In the case of event continuation, it is necessary to have prepared a standard act, which the event manager includes in the package of the documents, prepared for the event, in two copies. This separate act should specify to what hour the event is extended and how much additional monies should be paid. This addendum could be signed at the time of event.

All of the listed documents are used by the event manager. Some of them will be also used to address other units of the company. These must be prepared first in order to start the work of other units simultaneously. Therefore the functional sheet, ordered menu, plan of utility services room organization, and a common list of plating should be transferred for production.

The technical department should be sent the overview functional sheet, equipment-and-textile request, plan of utility services room organization, transport plan (if technical department is responsible for work with transport), the list of alcoholic beverages, soft drinks, and hot drinks, and the list of equipment rented from third-party contractors, when necessary.

At the commencement of the event's preproduction, it will be convenient and helpful to have a schedule of the equipment that is handed over to the personnel. The event manager or technical manager will record what was given to each employee and signed for. This helps in inventory return after work completion. An alternative to this can be customized cards of the waiters with the same information.

A company that develops good documentary forms to support the work of customer service managers and event managers will have a good tool for self-organization and self-control of personnel at time of work. These forms are also helpful with customers at the sales and event organization stages.

Documentary Forms for Working with Engaged Personnel

As already noted, the standard of catering company services largely depends on the presentation and ethic of the hired personnel. To eliminate common mistakes, implement a procedure of adding freelancers to the database that includes the following:

1. The information that is necessary to carry out the work. For example, does the freelancer own a spare coordinated outfit ("black bottom, white top")?
2. Information on stringent prohibitions. For example, there is no smoking while on duty.
3. Requirements in case of a plans change. It is necessary to document this information immediately and disseminate.
4. Information on exactly what duties are to be performed by all personnel in the process of event preparation. (For example, do the waiters' responsibilities include loading/unloading equipment, dish polishing, drapery and table settings, and so on?)
5. What are the functions of the staff during the event service (for example, dish renewal on buffet tables, collection of used crockery or banquet tables servicing)?
6. What are the staff functions *after* the event terminates (for example, the collection and packing of all equipment and similar)?
7. What is the payment policy? This should include a bonus plan, information about taxi payment for late nights, and so on.

8. The candidate should provide the following for inclusion in the database: full name, phone, clothing sizes, address, and so on.

Similarly, there should be a prepared standard for freelancers' callback:

1. Information on address, date, and time (with specification for morning/evening) of attendance
2. The information that is necessary for a staff person to carry (for example, ID, a set of clothes with specification of all its elements)
3. Detailed requirements as to the appearance of operating personnel, including acceptable hairstyle, makeup, jewelry, and so on.
4. Information on stringent prohibitions. For example, there is no smoking during the whole work time.
5. Work termination time and the possibility of overtime
6. Contacts of the manager to inform if the freelancer's plans changed and he or she will not be able to work at the event
7. Information as to the payment policy, including bonus plan, information about taxi payment for late nights, and so on

It is essential to describe a standard of instructions for engaged service personnel to carry out an event. There are three stages of instruction. General initial training takes place immediately before start of work. A secondary training occurs after completion of the preparation stage, shortly before the start of service. Lastly, any individual training of an employee takes place directly on the job site. General initial training of waiters is carried out after separation of the personnel per work zone and individual managers/supervisors. The following information should be included:

1. Receive assigned tasks, as well as responses to questions, from the manager or supervisor.
2. Upon completion of assignment, it is necessary to immediately submit the results to the manager/supervisor.
3. If a waiter needs to leave the position, it may only be by permission. The supervisor should be immediately informed upon return.
4. Food and drink may be ingested in the utility services room, at a break time that is provided by the manager/supervisor.
5. Establish a bonus system with the rules of bonus and possible reduction.

6. Establish the prohibition of smoking and drinking alcohol.
7. Establish the basis for accountability of loaned equipment unit.
8. An hour before the event, each employee will be assigned to a specific area of work.

Generally, the waiters' secondary instruction is held shortly before the start of the guest service. It should include the following information:

1. What is the service format and the protocol for renewal of all meals and drinks? Additionally, provide a detailed, step-by-step instruction on waiters' performance in the established service format.
2. Provide the information for all personnel groups that are responsible for different areas of work.
3. Instill a work ethic that prohibits the personnel from participating in the event beyond its service. Also require waitstaff to smile during the entire service.
4. Be especially clear as to the cleanliness requirements inclusive of personal appearance.
5. Provide instruction as to how a server is to answer the guests' questions.
6. Information about the meals should be disseminated inclusive of the dish name and its components. Also provide the schedule of course change. This will be provided to the supervisors in their areas of responsibility or to the manager.

Finally, the manager or supervisor that is dedicated to an area should carry out individual instructions in each. He or she repeats the basic rules of the project (read aloud during initial and secondary instructions), adjusts table settings, and gives individual comments as to the performance of each employee.

Other Types of Documentation

Besides documentary forms to support the work of the sales manager and event manager, we also recommend standardizing the work of the other functioning departments within the catering company. Develop databases of customers, freelance personnel, halls and sites, contractors, menus, equipment-and-textiles and so on.

Frequently, customers turn to catering companies when the event site has not yet been selected. They want to plan the menu and hear suggestions as to where to hold the event.

Practically all catering companies have a database of sites where they have already held events or potentially where events can be carried out. In smaller companies, the venue possibilities may be in a simple folder with separate sheets on which each site is described. To work with such minimal information is extremely inconvenient. Believe me, it is necessary to create the database of halls and sites in electronic form, in the form of a table. It should reflect this brief information about each venue:

- Title
- Exact address
- Brief description of the venue for the customer
- Venue representative with whom to interact on issues of lease of premises and the contact information
- Maximum capacity of the entire site for events in banquet/buffet/cocktail format
- Rental price and what is included in it
- Services that may be available for a separate charge (furniture, lighting, etc.)

Having this venue database enables a manager to quickly choose the most appropriate options for the customer.

The contractor database should include various categories such as transport companies, rental companies, decorative firms, agencies for temporary personnel, and so on. To have this separate database affords an optimal structure that is convenient and operational.

In the meal database, created in the form of a spreadsheet, it is necessary to input by course: salad, appetizer, hot appetizer, main meal, condiments or sauces, and dessert. Then include the name of the dish with a short "poetic" description of it. This may be inserted later into a formal menu. Include the meal's basic ingredients, the total yield of the course in grams, and its cost and sale value. If the company works with a standard menu, it is necessary to specify in which of them each meal is included (for example, "premium banquet," "optimum buffet," and "economy cocktail").

In the simplified approach, the company sends its full assortment list to the customer, upon request. I do not recommend this approach; it's not as effective and professional because it does not characterize the company itself. The customer may initially draw conclusions about the limitation of meal choices. A better, second option is the individualized menu that is developed for the customer. This requires a certain amount of time.

Consequently, after repeated preparation of each individual menu, a manager may think that he or she has a set routine. The manager has provided a good combination for any service format and will begin to apply previously used options. Eventually, the company's management supposedly assumes an individual approach to the customer but in reality, the managers work according to their own standard menu.

However, the work according to a developed standard menu is the third option. The customer is offered the choice of several standard menus, optimally designed for carrying out a particular format of service within time and budget. With this approach, the time for preparation of proposal and menus for each new customer is significantly reduced. Of course, few customers order a standard menu. In one way or another, he or she combines from various options offered and sometimes even adds something at his or her pleasure. Therefore, after a conversation with the customer, the manager has to adjust the proposed standard menu, which he or she takes as a basis for the new event. To be the most effective in dealing with the customer, it is not necessary to send more than two menu options.

Lots of companies offer a menu with no indication of the value of each meal included in its composition. They may indicate the value of the menu, based on one person, inclusive of delivery, service, and so on. Some companies point out the price of each meal separately and additionally prescribe the costs related to transport, service, and so on. Sometimes customers offer to reduce the number of personnel or discuss the transport services prices. In other words, the customer often wants to affect the pricing for event budget optimization. However, the customer will not bear any responsibility for result and level of service, if the catering company will settle for any crude compromises. If the customer accepts the bid, then the format of "one price" in the menu offer will be the best option. Of course, when individual customers require an entire structure of expenses in a commercial proposal, it is possible to do them a favor.

At the time of any changes made by the customer, the manager has a request for a new menu calculation. In the absence of an automated system (at least it can be arranged in simple Excel table), the manager will have to carefully rework the list of meals and redetermine their net cost and sale value, often with the involvement of the head chef. When a meal database exists, it should be specifically designed for the purpose of menu cost tabulating. Then a manager can quickly change all calculations at his or her discretion.

Catering companies are also faced with the need to use "documentary forms of accounting." These include forms for processing of income, inventory, and retirement of equipment (depot and production) and textiles (including decor and uniform), including textile turnover with a laundry services, as well as forms for accounting of balances and products retirement, drinks, and expendable materials. These are standard forms, and they do not differ from those that are used in traditional restaurants.

PART 4

Development of a Quality Control System

Standard of Service and Standardized Control Procedures

A system of operating standards for the company is absolutely essential for quality control management. This is individual to each catering company and can't be developed to be universally applicable.

When operating standards do not exist, quality is difficult to control. If a manager who deals with the preparation and management of events does the job only in accordance with his or her own vision, it is impossible to keep permanent quality of a company's work and objectively assess it.

It can often be heard from catering managers that everything is fine: their systems work properly and are well organized, and management is highly professional. And yet events aren't executed well. Sounds ridiculous, doesn't it?

Usually the problem is linked to the fact that the staff were not informed about the management's expectations or not provided with operating and service standards. In other words, they were not managed properly. As a result, waiters perform relying on their own vision of work, which may lead to reprimands or customer complaints.

The human factor is even more unreliable in catering as it involves a lot of outsourcing and temporary staff. That's why it is so crucial to develop unified company standards regarding what things should be done and how. For example, it can refer to service process standardization—what hand should a waiter carry a tray in, and so on? You can standardize a buffet table setting by pointing out where plates should be placed, their quantity, the location and order of flatware, and where spices and breadbaskets should be placed. A company that has introduced this kind of standard is not going to be dependent on the manager who is in charge of the event.

It is very dangerous to rely on staff professionalism to justify the absence of a standard operating system. In this case, quality disappears as experienced employees leave the company. In contrast, a company that has operating standards can control service quality, be highly reputable, and give the customers what they value so much—security and consistent quality.

When the standard exists, you can monitor how it is followed. Quality may be monitored by a department representative who visits the events with a certain frequency. He or she puts a plus or a minus in a service standard control form in front of brief phrases (stated in affirmative) because the standards are either followed or not. There is no prize for a "kind of" or "almost" followed the protocols. For example, the standard states that one to three piles of fifteen, twenty, and twenty-five plates should be placed on both ends of the buffet line. Any deviation from this rule can be considered a standard violation. Every properly written standard can be controlled by any person. But the absence of clear criteria—like in the phrase "there are piles of plates on the tables," when it is not stated how many plates are in each pile and/or how many piles are on the table and where they are to be located—makes the objective assessment of a standard impossible.

It is reasonable to introduce a system of subjective assessment to complement control of a service standard. In this case, a supervisor at the same time with objective standard assessment answers a list of "open questions." This type of form is based on a point system, from one to five, instead of a plus or a minus. If an area doesn't receive a five, it requires justification and comments. For example, you can assess in this system by "Friendliness of staff," "Condition of tablecloth," "Buffet line decoration," "Quality of technical space organization," and so on.

The system of subjective assessment is complementary to the system of standard control and allows us to evaluate aspects not listed in standards to achieve a broader outlook on company service. A key point in introducing the system of standards is to communicate to employees its goals. These goals are to maintain and improve the level of service. This system of standards and its monitoring should not become a tool of "searching and punishing the offenders." Instead it should uphold the standards and narrow down to formalities. In this way, one can ascertain why everything is seemingly performed correctly but the service still leaves much to be desired.

System of Control and Optimization of Functional Divisions

Operating standards can and should be used to optimize the work of the company's functional divisions.

The objects of control must first be identified. For instance, we can consider food and beverage purchase prices, regulations of covering the staffing needs (how many waiters and cooks must be involved in servicing this or that scale and type of event), and the technical provision of the event. After this, the standards must be established for every chosen object. For example, the number of cooks invited for servicing the buffet for one hundred persons must not exceed the number stated in the standard. As for purchase prices, when the budget is overdrawn, more additional coordination between the purchase department and financial manager is required. Regarding the technical provision of the event, the established standards are met in the situation when all requested equipment is delivered from the warehouse in complete accordance with the stock list and in quantity needed. Otherwise, the standards are not met.

After defining the objects of control and establishing their assessment standards, frequency and forms of control must be chosen. Purchase prices, for example, can be controlled once a quarter. Staff standards as well as technical provisions should be assessed once a month.

Next, we must define the way we receive customer feedback and the consequences of violating the standards.

Customer Feedback and Other Components of a Quality Control System

Customers can control a company's growth. We just need to know how to utilize their ideas. First of all, we can recommend developing a feedback form to track customer satisfaction. The responsibility of processing customer feedback as well as control of upholding standards can be taken by an owner, an event service department head, or, at best, by the quality control group represented by employees of different departments.

The form must be simple and convenient for customers to understand and fill out. It should reference specific work areas. It is crucial to ask questions in a correct way. For example, if you put a question like this—"Did you enjoy the service?" or "Would you use our service again?"—it may result in a brief negative response: "No." It would be difficult to identify the area that needs to be improved upon or take some exact measures to avoid customer dissatisfaction in the future. That is why every question should be well thought out and refer to a specific area of work. It is necessary to exclude general questions, whose answers cannot help to identify failing areas of the process.

You should give special thought to the method of getting customer feedback forms back to the customer. The best way would be to get the sales managers interested in the forms collection.

All the feedback must be precisely processed and analyzed. In small companies, this can be done by an owner. In larger firms, this analysis can be delegated, for example, to department heads.

The following list of questions can be used as a sample customer feedback form:

Event preparation phase

1. General impression of the company after the first call
2. Speed of sending a commercial offer
3. Commercial offer (how detailed and relevant?)
4. Professional competence and awareness of the manager
5. How customer-oriented is the manager?

Event running phase

6. Professionalism of the manager
7. Professionalism of the staff (waiters, bartenders)
8. Taste of the dishes
9. Plating of the dishes
10. Decoration of buffet/banquet tables
11. Arranging of banqueting facilities

You must also provide the customers the chance to give detailed comments:

12. What can we improve?
13. What do you like the most about our company?

The form must be easy and fast to fill in to increase the efficiency and customer's desire to complete it. For example, allow the customer to use a five-point grading scale for every question. The questions I have provided can be integrated into the operating standard system of a catering company and should be used as a tool of increasing a company's efficiency and providing permanent quality of service.

A quality control table can also be used for monitoring the quality of services given. This table can be filled in by event managers or customer service managers if their job descriptions combine sales and event running. In this case, this form can be even more efficient due to a higher level of motivation in increasing the quality of service among the employees involved in sales than among those dealing only with event running.

The truth is that event managers will not have to deal with customers in secondary sales, irrespective of high or low quality of service provided. In the quality control table, a manager leaves comments about all components of the service given. The date of the event, name of a customer company, and number of guests must be stated for every event. After that, a manager leaves his or her opinion about the menu and the cook's performance, the technical provision of the event, the labor of the technical department/warehouse/rental company, and the waiters' and even his or her own performance. For example, a manager can write in the form that this or that dessert was so-so, in his or her opinion. The manager may recommend that it should probably be excluded from the assortment or its recipe changed. A manager can also praise the technical department for excellent work and highlight that unloading was done quickly. A manager should be willing to fill in this form openly and honestly, once he or she realizes that these comments are an effective tool for improving the level of service rather than searching and punishing the guilty parties.

In regard to the introduction of these documents, it is worth noting that all of them must become an integral part of the work routine of every employee. In other words, if filling in the forms is only stated in the employee manual but not integrated as an essential part of the work routine, it can just be forgotten. Can you remember when the last time was you read your own employee manual and which of your duties you do on a regular basis?

Similar forms can be introduced for other employees in paper form as a kind of "quality notebook." I would recommend that for the wider range of employees, this is only introduced for a limited period of time. Such notebooks must be given to all the staff, including dishwashers, cooks, stewards, technical managers, etc. Suggest they be filled out at every event they work. Usually one month a year is enough. Obviously, you should not introduce this quality control tool in December when the intensity of work is at its peak. And you should write in capitals on its cover that nobody will be punished for his or her responses. Otherwise, this quality control tool will not work because of employees' apprehensions and unwillingness to talk about real problems and bottlenecks in the company's work.

Management Evaluations

Customer feedback, quality control tables, and quality notebooks help to control the quality at the event stage, whereas at the sales stage it is necessary to track the quality through evaluation of the manager's work efficiency: sales managers and customer service or project managers (if sales and event running functions are combined). You can use an easy statistical data for this. How many event service requests were made versus how many brought an actual contract? This is the easiest criterion.

When a manager works in reactive sales (does not actively look for or attract customers), you can count the proportion of customers becoming real out of potential and vice versa. Certainly, we should consider the fact that not every request is real, and there is some amount of incidental requests—for example, when a company gets a request about a delivery of a couple of dishes that is too small an order or a customer expects another price point. As a rule, such requests are eliminated at the first conversation between a manager and a potential customer. However, sometimes some really promising potential customers resort to competitors during the sales stage (additional coordination of commercial offer, choosing a banqueting space).

By evaluating catering companies working in megacities, with consideration of high competition, a normal manager is the one who turns one hundred potential requests into thirty real events. Such figures are typical for an active, motivated, and customer-oriented manager. If the number of real events is only fifteen, the efficiency of this manager should be paid attention to, because it is a low ratio.

When a manager works in proactive sales, we can count the number of contracts made as a result of proactive sales out of a total amount of requests. For example, thirty out of one hundred requests are turned into contracts, and three of them come from proactive sales; the rest are reactive. Finally, we get a result of 10 percent, which can be compared to the result of other managers in this department or the same manager in different periods. One more statistical criterion is the number of second sales out of the total. For example, five out of thirty events a manager had during the year were ordered by "old," loyal customers.

All three criteria can characterize the efficiency of the manager's work. The first indicates how many customers become real out of the total amount of potential. The second shows how good the manager is at proactive sales. And the third illustrates how many customers come back to this manager for repeat business.

After processing these and any other statistics, it is important to make them a tool to motivate managers to improve the quality of work. So the managers with the highest results should be fostered to motivate them and other employees to increase the result. Indeed, the level of service must be developed not only at the event stage but also at the sales stage. Quality in a manager's performance can and must be a part of the competitive advantage of a catering company!

PART 5

Opportunities for Promoting Catering Services and Selling Them to Corporate Customers

Possible Promotional Tools

Off-premises catering is first of all a *type* of service. This means that not all the tools that prove efficient in product promotion are suitable for service promotion.

Catering companies have tried all types of ads, including national TV, radio, and billboards, but only once. The conclusion seems clear: these types of ads don't work for catering service promotion. The return is quite low. Such advertising campaigns are mostly held by the companies servicing some public events organized by one of the media companies. Payment is usually done in a form of barter; in exchange for off-premises catering service, customers provide ad spaces or air time. As a rule, this type of reciprocal payment is only acceptable for big catering companies. Small companies usually only agree to partial barter payments, within the limits of 30–50 percent of total budget of the order. They prefer to get the net cost of their service in real payment.

This barter service allows both sizes of companies to receive promotion that is not planned for in their operating budgets. It provides an opportunity to be showcased at serviced events, which are often purely image building by themselves.

Since most companies are not ready to pay "real cash" for advertising on TV, radio, or outdoor ads due to the low return rate, what can be effective advertising for a catering company? The answer is easy and difficult at the same time: the same ads that can be efficient for any kind of service sales can be helpful to a catering concern. Moreover, we should remember that catering is to a much bigger extent a service for corporate customers—at least this segment is considerably larger than private customers.

Cold calls as an integral part of phone sales are traditionally used for catering service promotion. Sales managers call potential customers who have never requested any service in the company and therefore don't expect the call. That's why these are called "cold."

"Need a new customer? Call the old one!" is a principle that also works well in corporate sales. Keeping an old customer always costs less than attracting a new one. Marketing specialists say that attracting new customers is ten times more expensive than efforts spent on keeping old customers.

It is extremely important and efficient to build long-term, ongoing relationships with customers. It comes as no surprise that the term "follow-up" is so widely spread. This term is used in first conversation with a customer about a single order and in the long-term perspective.

In the first case, a manager calls a potential customer the next day after the customer received a commercial offer. The manager asks the questions: "Did you get our offer?" "Do you have any questions?" "Can we make it more attractive to you?" In taking this follow-up action, a manager doesn't allow the customer to forget about the offer and stays in touch to immediately react to any changes in plans. This also provides the chance to influence a situation when a customer is considering other competitive offers at the same time. This practice has proven that a customer, when choosing an outsourcer, is influenced by the customer service of a manager. It is by far one of the most important factors, after price level and reputation of the company.

A customer may choose an outsourcing company just due to the attentiveness of the manager who works with him or her and who sends offers, answers questions, and so on. It's very important to the customer as to how available a manager is and how quickly he or she takes calls and corrects commercial offers.

Long-term follow up requires maintaining and developing a relationship with a customer after the event is over. A manager may call in some time and remind the customer about the company's service and ask about future plans. This scenario where a manager makes follow-up calls is the simplest but not the most efficient form of contact used in phone sales. Hence, sometimes an indirect follow up is used when a manager doesn't discuss possible sales with the customer directly but speaks about different, unrelated matters that are of interest to both. This may be considered a more progressive form of staying in touch with customers. The main objective is to remind the customer about your company, without any pressure or negatives that usually occur in response to regular service offer calls.

We recommend "partnership marketing" as marketing research in any sphere. In this case, a company contacts real and potential customers without offering service but just asking them to act as partners and give some recommendations. This way, you can achieve two goals in one. The first is to collect information to improve the level of customer service. The second is to remind the customers about the company and its service. You may address the customers with a wide variety of questions: "We are updating operating standards, and we'd like to know what is important to you when you work with catering company," or "We are preparing a new seasonal menu, and we'd like to ask what you would prefer in a New Year's menu." You can also add that the most detailed and informative answer will be awarded with a present—for example, a house special set of desserts. If you manage to get feedback, you can hand in the data for analysis to the marketing department. As a rule, the proportion of customers who agree to answer is quite low, usually 3–5 percent. Even in the absence of any considerable customer feedback, this method reminds the former customer about your company's existence. In awarding a winner, a company can be brought to the customers' attention again, if the information about the winner will be sent to all participants of a survey. By the way, it's a great idea to present this information as news on your company website. This indicates the activity of the company, its motivation to improve the level of service, and its creative approach to cooperation with customers.

Large catering companies should also use other divisions for promotion. For example, place different booklets, banners, and other media advertising the firm in a chain of cafes belonging to a concern. Additionally, the company can offer discount loyalty cards to big customers or other holding services.

The topic of "strategic alliances" deserves special attention. There are enough companies, of a different business profile, working in the event servicing market that are not direct competitors of catering companies. They are event agencies, decoration companies, light and sound equipment suppliers, rental companies, and so on.

By allying with one or more of these market players, a company can create a so-called strategic alliance. Why is it necessary? First of all, every participant of this alliance gets an extra sales channel for its services. Moreover, in partnership with other companies, a catering company can offer its service on a brand-new level. For example, there was a situation when one quite famous multinational sent a request to one company for a New Year's party for a hundred people announcing a budget of $500 per person. This sounded quite attractive, even for a premium segment. The customer requested not only catering but a full-scale service including event organizing, banquet space decoration, and an entertainment program. This was all presented as one conceptual event, where all elements of a reception were integrated. So the customer went to the competition because the catering company didn't have a stable partner relationship with any event agencies at that time. And the order, by the way, was given to the competitor by the partner event agency. Anyway, the company learned the importance of collaboration between event agencies and catering. A year later, the same big company came to them again; they didn't lose the opportunity and managed to offer a full-scale service for organizing and servicing their conceptual event by using the resources of strategic alliance.

So companies joining in strategic alliances can recommend each other as reliable partners when customers ask for relevant services. They can also offer all-inclusive product—for example, conceptual parties with topical menus: "Sweet Life, or Dipped in Chocolate" or "Black and White, or 101 Dalmatians." Companies can announce their partnerships on their websites, commercial offers, and ad materials. There is also the possibility to place common ads in printed and Internet media. These are all possibilities for optimizing advertising budgets. The biggest benefit to every company within an alliance is an additional sales channel through the partners.

Alliances have other advantages too. For example, before the demand for New Year's parties, partners can organize common advertising campaigns. As a rule, they are not cheap, so it's a rational decision to share costs with partners. What's more, customers will definitely appreciate that a catering company doesn't do everything indiscriminately—only the things included in its area of professional competence. More than one-third of orders come from event agencies, not directly from customers. Additionally, the budget per person in these "agency" events is often higher than in events from "direct" customers. This is due to the fact that customers who aim to work with event agencies are usually ready to spend more for every separate service, including catering.

Apart from some evident benefits of strategic alliances, there are others you should learn about. First of all, at the start of cooperation, both sides must clearly negotiate terms, conditions, and patterns of interaction. It's important to understand that the main goal of companies is to increase, not decrease, the range of possibilities of service promotion. It means that neither a catering company nor an event agency exclude the chance to work with other partner-competitor companies. In other words, the companies will have the same opportunities on the market that they had before joining the alliance. But they will become strategic partners and mutually provide service more intensely.

Catering companies often use different mailing services (e-mail, direct mail) for promoting their services. However, every year they become less and less efficient. It is crucial that you not send out "junk mail" that is immediately thrown into the wastebin. Endeavor to present your advertising message in a creative way to capture customer attention. Sometimes restaurants send customers not only advertising booklets but lists of original recipes. Given that most representatives of companies are women, it can be quite a meaningful and efficient message. There was one unusual story when a company put a real one-dollar banknote in the envelope with an advert. Customers paid attention to these mails, remembered the company, and told their acquaintances about it.

In print advertising, PR articles in image periodicals and adverts in industry-specific periodicals for HR departments and marketing specialists tend to be the most effective.

The most promising and convenient, for efficiency tracking, is online context and banner advertising. Some companies make SEO promotion their only promotional tool.

Bonus and discount systems can also become a good addition for catering service promotion. We must remember the first rule of marketing: every discount is valid only for a limited period of time. Termless discounts are just a decrease of price. You should first of all understand what a company achieves by offering a discount. Discounts can be efficient for large-scale events (for example, over three hundred people). You can also give seasonal discounts like "November discount" or "first quarter discount" when the intensity of work is not at its peak. A discount for loyal customers, who return within one year, is also good. As previously mentioned, it's easier to keep old customers than attract new.

There are different opinions on what proportion the advertising budget should be relative to total amount of sales. These figures vary from 2 to 10 percent. In fact, the most important thing to remember is that it's better to be guided by the aims and ambitions of the company in the market and not by the postulates of unknown "experts."

The Components of a Commercial Offer to Corporate Customers

A considerable faction of potential customers makes decisions to hire a catering company at the stage of receiving a commercial offer. This phase has its peculiarities in regard to corporate customers. What does it consist of?

A private customer planning some event (wedding, birthday party, anniversary) typically comes to the restaurant in person to discuss the details and get answers from a restaurant manager. This is vastly different with corporate customers. Negotiations with an outsourcer (in this case, a restaurant or a catering company) are led by a middle manager, and decisions are made by bosses. For this reason, it's not enough just to answer the questions when working with corporate customers. It's essential to prepare a written commercial offer so that a manager can show it to top management. We should remember that corporate customers are hardly ever limited to considering just one commercial offer of a service supplier. It's twice as important to make your written commercial offer detailed, qualitative, and at the same time brief and "readable." Moreover, it should be competently composed to make a customer understand, even in the early stages, how professional this potential outsourcer is.

After receipt of a request for a commercial offer, a sales manager should get to work. At this stage, the presence of a basic structure of a commercial offer can be used as a pattern, which spares a manager from writing every passage from scratch. I can suggest the following basic structure of written commercial offer (with a menu included):

- Document header contains a logo, name, and contacts of a catering company.
- List the contact information of the customer the commercial offer is addressed to: name of the company, name and surname of a contact person, phone number, and e-mail.
- Introductory passage with greetings and brief information about the request—for example, "Dear Karen, as per our telephone conversation, I'm sending you a commercial offer regarding catering service for your upcoming event for 250 people, on December 23 from 6:00 p.m. to midnight in the photo gallery on Sunset Boulevard." This passage can be useful for the catering service manager, who can quickly get any key data about any coming event just by opening one of the commercial offers in process.
- A list of competitive advantages of the company. Highlight some points in favor of choosing your company as an outsourcer. Since there is growing competition in the catering industry, you should make it clear to the customer why you are the right company to work with. You can provide the following facts: how long the company has worked in the off-premises catering market, what discount system it has, what famous clientele a company has previously worked with, and so on.
- A description of banqueting spaces for this event with the rental price. It's not worth offering two or three options. Catering companies logically don't include this passage in commercial offers for event agencies. It's necessary when working directly with a customer. Even with an individual, it doesn't pay to offer more than two or three venues, as customers expect to get only the most suitable options.
- Menu and everything connected with the food offer. Add comments to the offered menu regarding what is included in the price and what can be offered for additional payment. Here you can discuss a possibility of meeting guests, special buffet dishes, making a holiday cake, and so on.
- Drinks should be included in the offer: alcohol, soft drinks, hot drinks, etc. Provide a price list of all drinks in this paragraph. Additionally, you can define the amount of "corkage fee," on the condition that a customer uses his or her own alcohol. But at a primary offer, it's better to be limited by drinks list.
- Table decoration should be included in the offer for off-premises catering. Companies often neglect the question of table decoration. You should consider corporate colors of a customer company, topical aspect of the event,

and style of chosen banqueting space when decorating the tables. Table settings may be livened up with help of natural flowers, fabric draperies, candles, glass, mirrors, iron accessories, and so on. Leading companies are ready to offer customers several variants to the basic table setting included in the price. The description of these variants should be included in this paragraph of the commercial offer. Further, you should state other options that may be ordered (e.g., live floral arrangements) and their additional costs.
- Extra services: entertainment programs, MCs, lights, sound, stage equipment rentals, and so on. Huge companies try to avoid incidental work, but for small companies, such optional services can be an extra source of profit.
- Technical details can include the size of banqueting tables, color of drapery, time necessary for preparation and finishing the event, etc.
- Conclusion of a commercial offer—for example, "Let us know if we can make our offer more attractive to you. We are ready to answer all your additional questions. Sincerely yours, Ian Wight."

A commercial offer written according to this pattern can consist of more than three pages. This means that not all customers will read it in full. It is a point in your favor to pay special attention to how well-structured and illustrative the offer is, as well as to its visual presentation and visual highlighting of every paragraph.

Both off-premises catering and traditional restaurant businesses permanently work with specific brands of food and drinks. Therefore, you must necessarily state these brands in a commercial offer. Why? A customer may have something to do with these brands or have strategic partners linked with some food or drink brands. For example, McDonald's uses only soft drinks produced by Coca-Cola at all corporate and other events. Moreover, a customer's company can take into account its invited VIP guests who are somehow connected with brands. Different brands of drinking water, coffee, and juices can serve as an example. You can't foresee 100 percent when using certain brands may be problematic. So the best way out is to state every brand of drinks used in a commercial offer. It's especially timely in a situation when communication between a customer and a catering company is complicated—for example, in the case of when nondirect sales are involved or when working in collaboration with an event agency who acts as the main outsourcer in charge of an event.

Organizing Testing Events

It is very common that customers request a tasting of all dishes included in the offered menu. This is an opportunity to gain favor with a potential customer over another outsourcer. Testing is usually held after considering and selecting several potential outsourcers. Typically, two companies with comparable service and price points are under consideration. Therefore, it is difficult to give a preference to either company. A customer needs some additional criteria to make a choice and asks for a demonstration to determine which company will work better for him or her.

If a catering company works on the premises of a stationary restaurant or a hotel, it seems reasonable and easy to invite a customer for a testing. Undoubtedly, work in a stationary restaurant and off-premises catering are two different things. This is why many experienced customers don't agree to restaurant testing and give preference to the off-premises catering format. Therefore, testing is often held in an office of a customer or at the event agency. This allows a catering company to prepare all the dishes in the approved menu, deliver all equipment (furniture, fabric, dishes, etc.) and products, and serve tables in the off-premises format. As a result, a customer evaluates not only the quality of food and appearance of dishes but also the appearance of the waiter (who will be certainly involved in testing), the table setting and drapery, and the quality of dishes and equipment.

Testing is not always aimed at choosing the right outsourcer and checking quality of cuisine. Sometimes even loyal customers demand testing before every event. It's done to approve the content of the menu "in reality." In this case, a catering company intentionally serves a larger amount of dishes, since in process of testing some of the dishes may be eliminated as unsuitable. This approach to testing is typical for all premium customers and events.

Basic Rules and Practical Recommendations for Organizing Testing Events

There are some profound principles necessary for testing. First of all, testing can be held only after a customer *approves* the menu offered to him or her.

Nothing will be tested without an approval of a menu, since it is impossible to guess the food preferences of a customer. It's impossible to check the quality of dishes without this, because the dishes served at a caterer's own discretion can turn out to be something that customers "don't eat." Such dishes will not be appreciated even at their highest level. That's why only dishes acceptable to a customer can be tested. Also, a representative from the customer who approved the menu should take part in testing. Imagine a situation where a company head coordinated all his or her wishes about the menu for an upcoming New Year's company party and has chosen familiar dishes of traditional cuisine but due to scheduling can't take part in the actual testing. The head asks some employees and heads of different departments to take part in his or her stead. So five people enter a meeting room at the arranged day and time, where a catering company has prepared the approved menu. They are very disappointed when they don't see any foie gras, lobsters, or oysters on the offered menu. It's not easy to guess that their feedback about the cuisine's quality leaves much to be desired. In case of the company head's presence, any negative reaction of the employees could be transformed into updates to the menu. The testing would just fill in some clarifications and menu corrections, not a loss of the event. Therefore, the menu can be tasted only after preliminary approval on paper and with the obligatory presence of the person who approved it.

A catering company's manager in charge plays a key role in the process of testing. A manager's role consists of overseeing the entire process and guiding a customer. It's important that all represented people test all dishes included in the menu and provide their opinions about them in the following variants:

- Absolutely like the dish. Leave it on the menu.
- Don't like the dish. It's necessary to exclude or replace it.
- In general, it's acceptable for some changes to be made in the content or technology of cooking.

A manager should talk to customer's representatives about the menu before the tasting. Any changes offered regarding this or that dish can be discussed only in measurable categories. For example, some ingredients can be added or excluded, or their quantity or form of slicing can be changed.

Similarly, we can discuss corrections in plating, presentation, and the manner in which the dishes are served. But there are things that are impractical to discuss: the content of salt in smoked salmon or the amount of vinegar in marinated mushrooms. In fact, a batch of salmon, even from the same supplier, can be different by the time of an event. In this case, a company will not be immune from dissatisfaction regarding saltiness of the salmon even after all the previous coordination of the menu including smoked fish. The truth is that there won't be any chance to objectively compare the quality of salmon at the tasting and the event. Due to this reality, a manager should explain to the audience that only measurable and clear changes of dishes—that which can be controlled by a customer or a catering company—are going to be discussed.

Regarding the technology of cooking, professional catering companies can cook everything at the event identically to what was cooked for the testing. A catering service manager should also remind the participants at the testing that there will be more people with different eating preferences at the event, so they shouldn't project their own individual tastes on the proposed menu. The person who authorizes the payment counts the most. Apart from this, it would probably be right to consider eating preferences of a "typical guest" at a coming event. For example, if an event is planned for a logistics company where 80 percent of employees are porters, it would be a good idea to take their tastes into consideration and invite one shift leader.

The optimal number of participants for a testing is four to five people. Their opinions will be generalized into one common idea of a menu for the coming event. I know of a testing where thirty reps attended. It wasn't another event under the guise of testing. They all really discussed the content of the menu and technical details of plating and service. Certainly, all participants of the testing must have decision-making power, at least regarding the menu.

If an event agency is involved, one of the participants in the testing must be its rep. Different sexes of participants is an extra advantage because the tastes of different groups of an event count. In planning a testing, a catering company should prepare the approved menu for one more person than the number of reps because the catering company manager running the testing should be able to discuss content and taste characteristics of dishes.

Usually testing takes no less than two hours, although there are examples when company reps come and give recommendations regarding the menu without testing any dishes. It's expedient to print out an individual menu for every participant so that during the tasting every participant can make his or her own remarks. A catering company manager records all the comments and wishes and should try to narrow them down to excluding, replacing, or approving the dish, or making some changes (in measurable categories). In this way, on the next day a manager is able to present a customer with an updated menu addressing all wishes. The price of an updated menu should also be corrected.

We should discuss whether a testing should be paid or free. There are three considerations. If a catering company has some doubts about the seriousness of a customer, it's better to offer a paid testing. This way, expenses are minimized when a contract seems unlikely. The same decision should be made when a catering company itself is not so interested in a customer—for example, if the event is too small or low budget.

When a company is highly interested in a customer or very confident in its "powers," it is more likely to offer a free testing banking on future compensation of expenses, in case of a signed contract. There is another variant: offer a customer a conventionally free testing. It means that a customer and a catering company make a preliminary agreement on event servicing, and a customer makes a partial prepayment. If a customer refuses the catering service, the cost of testing will be retained from this prepayment (which usually equals a price of testing). If a customer prefers to continue the collaboration, the testing will be free, and the partial prepayment will be included in a total price of the event.

It's worth noting that free testing is a widely acknowledged norm for premium-class catering companies. This is absorbed by higher profit margins in this segment and the specific business profile of a customer who seeks the services of premium companies.

Catering companies don't have to count the price of every testing individually for each customer because testing expenses are not dependent on menu variations very much. This price can be universal, let's say, for four people. The price of the menu remains virtually unchanged because cost estimates consist of various components including delivery, waiter's salary, and so on. These components remain the same independent of menu content yet at the same time make even a bigger contribution to the price of testing than at a real event. A waiter who will serve eight to eighteen people at the event will serve only four or five people at testing. A van, which is large enough to deliver all the necessary things for an event for fifty to one hundred people, will be used only for testing for four or five people.

How We Can Help a Customer to Review Our Work Positively

The main task of a catering company's sales manager is in assuring a customer of the professionalism and reliability of the company. It's important not only to attract a customer but to avoid unconstructive attempts to control your work in further collaboration. So it's important for a manager to help a customer to ask the right questions. The answers to these will really help customers make the right conclusions about the quality of service.

For example, customers often try to ascertain the reliability and level of service of a company by asking questions like, "Is the food tasty?" "Do you have clean tablecloths?" and "Aren't you chair coverings rumpled?" What kind of answer can a manager give to these questions? When communicating with such a customer, a manager will have to ask constructive "right" questions and answer them on his or her own too. So a manager should describe the following things. What quantity of all dishes a company brings per person? How many waiters should be involved, and what areas of work they are going to be responsible for? What time should the company arrive at the banqueting space for preparation to the event?

With all this detailed information, a customer receives a better understanding of the level of offered service and convinces the customer of the reliability and professionalism of a prospective outsourcer. Moreover, real customer testimonials also very convincing. Documentation and all necessary certificates also confirm the professionalism and solid reputation of the company. Some catering companies have a so-called showroom: a hall where all the patterns of banquet furniture, dishes, tableware, drapery textiles, staff uniforms, and decoration elements are on display. Such "visuals" convince customers of the seriousness and professionalism of a catering company. They also simplify negotiations over decoration and accessories for the coming event. This is a typical element for caterers in the premium segment. It's also convenient for them because it helps the customer to select appropriate collections of dishes for high-level events, while simpler collections are used in basic offers.

Taking advantage of an additional opportunity at the sales stage, a manager can invite a potential customer to the "battleground"—to another event catered by the company. Naturally, this visit can be organized only before the start of the event and before the arrival of guests. If that isn't convincing enough, a manager can offer a customer a testing. So involving a wide variety of points in favor of his or her offer, a manager simultaneously convinces a customer of the solidness of the catering company and demonstrates a high level of service. This provides the customer a chance to make a choice based on real facts.

PART 6

The Requisite Equipment for Catering

In order to provide efficient catering and services to a broad range of events in a timely and professional manner, it is necessary to acquire a certain set of catering equipment. First of all, one must have the processing equipment. This includes thermal, refrigeration, and neutral hardware for the production facility, typically called the kitchen facility. Second, as opposed to traditional restaurants, catering calls for mobile equipment to serve off-site events. This includes the furniture, crockery, tableware and utensils, tablecloths, and so on. Other equipment is required as well.

There are several approaches to building a catering business. The most sound approach, whether for a stationary restaurant or an independent, dedicated catering company, involves building production capacities on a base of processing equipment.

A catering kitchen should be outfitted with the same set of equipment as the kitchen of a stationary restaurant, with one considerable distinction: because of high food processing volumes in catering, only high-efficiency, multifunctional equipment is used. This is in order to conduct various processing steps to prepare a broad range of dishes. It includes combi steamers, multiburner stoves, batch cookers, tilting pans, combo frying surfaces, cold pans, and rapid-cooling and shock-freezing chambers. It goes without saying that a growing catering facility that deals with smaller events can start with more basic equipment.

After meal preparation, the next step is delivery to the event, in a presentable condition and according to health and safety regulations. The equipment for food transportation must maintain the temperature of above 149°F (65°C) for hot dishes and under 45°F (7°C) for cold dishes. One way to accomplish this is in the use of stainless steel or polycarbonate Gastronorm containers, which are then placed in thermal containers that guarantee food quality over a protracted period of time without losing visual appeal.

The Processing Equipment

In order to optimize costs, it is necessary to simplify and standardize all food processing steps. Largely, this is achieved by utilizing thermal equipment composed of individual modules. The section module approach to equipping thermal lines allows optimal configurations of various modules: stoves, cookers, pans, boilers, deep fryers, grills, braziers, steam tables, and so on. On the whole, it increases overall productivity due to a use of kitchen space. Additionally, the functional choice of containers for storage, processing, and transportation of meals can further contribute to a more optimal use of section module equipment.

The first item a catering business must acquire is a stove(s) for boiling, frying, stewing, and sautéing of large volumes of food. For the sake of economics, it is practical to buy a stove that has six or eight separate burners. To significantly increase the amount of cookery that is in use simultaneously, as well as to expand the assortment of meals, use a stove with a continuous surface and multiple heating areas.

In certain cases, instead of electric stoves, it is preferable to use gas ranges that can use not only mainstream pipeline gas but also canister fuel in case of emergency. A gas stove heats food much faster than an electric one, reducing the time it takes to prepare meals. Gas is more efficient as one can quickly change the intensity of the flame, effectively controlling the heat output. It is possible to significantly speed up the processing time by using continuous-surface stoves, instead of a stove with open burners, where cookware of varying sizes can be placed simultaneously.

Induction ovens, which do not require preheating and consume less electricity, are considered more compact and technically advanced. For a variety of Asian dishes, it is recommended to buy a stove that can accommodate deep, round vessels with convex bottoms of small diameter, such as woks. An induction stove does not release heat into the atmosphere and has a broad output range that allows for cooking dishes at various degrees of heating.

For standardization of workflow, it is recommended to acquire a stove that has an oven, which is ideal for preparing large banquet dishes or baked goods. Buy one equipped with detachable rails on the side walls to support grids and standard Gastronorm containers type GN1/1 and GN2/1. The most suitable are ovens with forced movement of the heating medium, such as water steam or heated air. Ideally, an oven should have separate output controls for each group of heating elements. Some models of convection ovens also include the function of moistening, which is essential for baking fermented dough.

Boilers are indispensable for boiling vegetables and large volumes of water. To save kitchen space and electricity, it is sensible to buy multifunctional models—for example, a boiler with two separate vessels in one frame so two different dishes can be prepared simultaneously. Or purchase a model that has a mixer function and can rapidly cool prepared dishes with a trip mechanism. Such a boiler is suitable for preparing not only broth but also sauces, mashed potatoes, dough, and vegetable and fruit puree. The mixing function allows you to reduce the processing time since a uniform temperature is maintained in the boiler, while avoiding overcooking.

To fry meals, an electric pan with a stationary bed is required. It also saves on a purchase of a griddle plate. Such pans, with a flat, ruffled, or combined surface with separate heating areas, allow preparation of dishes in different vessels that require various degrees of heat. As a result, it is possible to find the right measure of heat for each individual dish. For stewing, poaching, and sautéing, a tilting pan is required. It easily prepares liquid dishes, such as sauces and broths. The mechanism of lifting and tilting the pan helps to reduce the time to empty it.

When the menu includes Mediterranean dishes, a pasta cooker is requisite in order to prepare macaroni, noodles, and spaghetti.

A deep fryer is required to prepare culinary and baked dishes fried in deep fat, such as french fries, meat and fish, doughnuts, and so on. To cater events with a smaller menu, a traditional model is suitable, with grated baskets that hold ingredients loaded into two fry vats. When the fryer has a mechanism that automatically lowers and lifts the baskets, it speeds up processing time. More advanced is the technology of pressure frying, when the foods are placed in preheated fat and hermetically sealed. Due to a shorter exposure to oil and higher steam pressure caused by the evaporating liquids inside, products retain natural flavor and juiciness. This allows expansion of the menu (by adding chicken, turkey, and fish), increases the output, and reduces electricity and oil consumption.

To prepare a broad range of dishes with diverse flavors, it is necessary to purchase a noncontact salamander grill. The heat is conducted by infrared radiation from above, and the heat intensity is regulated by changing the distance between the mobile heating surface above and the stationary surface with the product below. Such grills are ideal for preparing meat, poultry, or fish filets cooked to order, or juliennes and casseroles. To simultaneously fry a product from both sides, a contact grill such as a panini grill would be required. When a food product is placed between two heating elements, processing time and electrical consumption are both reduced.

Another piece of essential kitchen equipment is a combi steamer that combines a steam cooker with a convection oven. The technology marries circulating hot air and generated steam within one chamber. This allows any type of thermal conditioning and also significantly speeds up processing time. With the flexibility to regulate the temperature and humidity in the chamber, a cook can fully control such meal characteristics as the color, the juiciness, and the cooking time. This frees the kitchen personnel from monotonous routine work and allows them to focus more on food presentation. A combi steamer reduces electrical consumption by 60 percent, water consumption by 40 percent, and the cooking time by 30–50 percent. Depending on the configuration, the chamber can accommodate four, six, ten, or twenty Gastronorm vessels of type GN1/1. For catering needs, it is advisable to give preference to the more efficient models that accommodate ten or twenty vessels. If the menu includes dishes of a delicate consistency, such as seafood or baked goods, it is the best to use the delicate setting (low-temperature steam). The models that have twenty loading settings should ideally have a steam generator that would guarantee stable humidity inside. In such ovens, water is supplied under pressure from the pipe into a boiler with a heating coil. There it boils and generates steam that is gradually released into the chamber through a special valve.

It is particularly important to ensure consistent quality of the dishes when catering to a massive number of guests. That is why it is recommended to buy a combi steamer with a programmable control panel that can store multiple recipes and can keep track of various parameters such as the duration of a stage, turning humidification on and off, the temperature inside the chamber, rotation rate of the turbine, and so on.

A combi steamer helps to effectively resolve issues of time gaps between producing and serving the meals, which are so common in catering. With the help of blast chilling (for ready meals) or shock freezing (for intermediate goods), it minimizes the time the products are exposed to the environment. The technology moves the goods after thermal processing in the oven into the freezing chamber, where blast chilling reduces the temperature from 176°F (80°C) to 37°F (3°C) in 1.5 hours. Shock freezing goes from 176°F (80°C) to −0.4°F (−18°C) in 4 hours. After this, all it takes to serve the dishes is to warm them up to the desired temperature. This is achieved by moving them back into the combi steamer in regeneration mode.

To ultimately simplify the kitchen workflow, products and ready meals are placed in Gastronorm containers, which in turn are placed in mobile sliding racks. This allows for products to be moved from the precook shop to the hot shop on a cart and loaded into a processing device without rearranging. Using sliding racks to cool or warm up plated dishes becomes useful during catered events. For large events, not only combi steamers but also regenerators can be used to reheat frozen dishes in plates or Gastronorm containers to the desired temperature without losing their natural flavor, color, and aroma.

The size of the free-standing shock freezing chamber should match that of the combi steamer. Internal volume and the railings of this chamber should support both Gastronorm (530 by 325 millimeters) and baker (600 by 400 millimeters) trays. For fast and convenient operation, sliding carts can be used to move vessels from the ovens into the freezing chamber.

A stationary kitchen calls for various other freezing equipment. First of all, one needs medium-temperature chambers 30°F–72°F (0°C–8°C) for short-term storage of frozen dishes ready to be served. Also needed are low-temperature chambers from 10.5°F to 72°F (from -12°C to -22°C) for storing frozen products prior to thermal processing. For spatial efficiency and optimal cooking workflow, I recommend purchasing refrigerated tables with freezing chambers under the tabletop. These tables can be used not only to cut raw ingredients and prepare salads but also to store dishes short term. The tabletop's refrigerated surface reduces the risk of the foodstuff developing any microflora. It also helps to retain the food's attractive presentation and flavor profile. By purchasing refrigerated tables, a catering company that serves small events can effectively save on a freezing chamber purchase.

Equipment for Transportation of Dishes, Furniture, and Tableware

The catering business necessitates extensive use of specialized equipment for transportation of finished dishes. First of all, thermoboxes are required for transportation of liquid, baked dishes and desserts. The thermobox is a Gastronorm container that maintains the temperature of it's content for several hours. Depending on the range of supported temperatures, thermoboxes can be neutral, heated, or cooled. The temperature of hot dishes should not dip below 149°F (65°C), and cold dishes should not exceed 45°F (7°C) during transportation.

To maintain an optimal temperature during transportation and while catering an event, thermoboxes are required. Naturally, they are most efficient only for the first few hours, and then the temperature declines. This must be taken into account while catering.

When thermoboxes are used for the delivery of prepared meals to a catered event, it is absolutely essential to plan how long it will take between the cooking and the arrival at the event for service to the guests. This primarily applies to hot appetizers, main dishes, and sides. There are even examples (albeit they should only be counted as extreme compromises) when hot appetizers and main dishes with sides were transported in a chilled state in Gastronorm containers and later heated in chafing dishes or even electric stoves or ovens brought to a particularly large event. Many readers might react critically to the concept of transporting hot meals in a chilled state for future heating in such simplified conditions without a regeneration oven. Evidence indicates that it might not be possible to avoid reheating even when using thermoboxes.

This is why catering companies that work in the economy or middle market do not always splurge on thermoboxes. Instead, they use chafing dishes that heat meals directly at the buffet table or, at larger events, in the technical room.

Catering companies in the premium segment purchase combi steamers, regeneration ovens, and various other types of ovens. These increase the cost of mobile and stationary equipment but allow for cooking or reheating meals directly at the catered event location. Premium companies may also use various (exotic for middle market) equipment, such as heated plate dispensers.

To transport prepared meals, use standardized Gastronorm containers that meet food safety regulations, such as stainless steel AISI 18/10 or food plastic (polycarbonate or polypropylene) containers GN1/1, 1/2, 1/3, 1/4, 1/6, 1/9, 2/1, 2/3 that can endure temperatures ranging from −10°F (−40°C) to 250°F (120°C).

There are two conceptually different approaches to catering staff organization, which affects the way ready meals are transported to the buffet events. Some caterers, upon preparing the meals, transport them to the event location where the cooks plate and prepare them to be served. The second approach is to plate the dishes at the kitchen and then transport them in plastic food wrap to the event location on carts. With this approach, there is no need for the cooks to attend the actual event.

For catering, there is also a need to transport china and glass tableware such as cups, plates, wineglasses, dessert bowls, and so on. Typically, storage and transportation equipment for tableware is a plastic case with internal partitions for plates and cups. Originally, these cases were designed for use in dishwashers, but over time they were successfully adapted for the catering industry. Of course, they can also be used for the original purpose: to load tableware in dishwashers.

The number of partitions in a case can vary to fit glasses of different sizes, from shot glasses to large brandy snifters or ice cream bowls. The cases can easily be loaded on a rolling cart for convenient transportation and to save time and space. You can also buy a vinyl cover for the cart to protect it from dirt. As a result, you will have a compact mobile system for storing and transporting tableware.

It is important to mention that mobile equipment degrades much faster in catering than it does in a restaurant. It necessitates selecting and sometimes even designing and producing a variety of packaging for the entire assortment of the mobile equipment, such as tableware and serving equipment (chafing dishes and such). Premade plastic packages can be hit or miss. For example, many catering companies use plastic containers originally intended for transportation of vegetables to transport plates. This is far from ideal because the only safe way to transport plates is edgeways, which is not possible in a vegetable container. In contrast, it is easy to find a container to transport silverware. Of course, improvised containers only work with more standard equipment or tableware. When expensive tableware sets are utilized, it calls for more careful packing and transport.

Some caterers use specialized equipment for transportation of furniture, such as carts for folding chairs and tables. At the same time, caterers in the economy or middle market simply use folding tables and stackable chairs that are hidden from the guests' eyes under fabric covers.

Therefore, there are many different options to select transportation equipment for companies that work in different price segments. This is why there is not one norm in catering. What is normal for one caterer should not be taken as a rule for others. What is reasonable in the premium segment would be a waste of money in the economy segment. What is a compromise in the economy segment would not be acceptable in the premium class.

The Equipment for Serving, Decorating, and Other Purposes

It is rare that catering companies have a need for thermal from 86°F to 194°F (30°C to 90°C) or chilled from 30°F to 50°F (−2°C to 10°C) salad bars, which are essentially tables with built-in basins for Gastronorm containers 4 to 6 GN1/1. Salad bars placed against the wall or as an island in the middle of a catering hall not only effectively showcase the meals but also help with short-term storage and service. However, this equipment is not particularly popular among caterers due to its bulky size and difficulty to transport.

According to sanitary regulations, hot items (soups, sauces, and drinks) must be served at the temperature not below 168°F (75°C); main dishes and sides should not be served below 149°F (65°C). To maintain unplated dishes in a hot state of 131°F–176°F (55°C–80°C) for two to three hours during a buffet event, steam tables and chafing dishes are used. Steam containers are made of chrome-plated or polished stainless steel. The heating is conducted with the help of electricity or burners with gel or dry fuel.

Chilling the dishes is accomplished by using chillers (also known as ice accumulators). Although not used very often, this equipment helps to keep meals cold in hot weather, indoors or in open air. Chillers generate cold due to ice that accumulates on the surface of an evaporator in a thermally insulated container with water. During the rapid melting of ice, at peak thermal pressure, water is released at a temperature of about 32°F (1°C) that is subsequently used to chill the dishes. The difficulty in using this equipment at buffet events is that the water pipes need to be disguised with fabric or other accessories. This doesn't fit the current trend of "light" catering decor.

Besides, chillers require electricity so, along with electric chafing dishes, they are not commonly used at catered events.

Regarding electricity, what else consumes power at catered events, and what does a caterer do if it's not available? First of all, electricity is needed in order to cook and reheat meals, so when it is not available, thermoboxes or chafing dishes are used in lieu of combi steamers and ovens. That is why any catering company should possess or rent equipment to work in various conditions. Electricity is needed for hot beverages such as tea and coffee. Therefore, when coffee machines are not available, hot beverage containers such as thermoses are required. To chill cold and alcoholic beverages when cold chambers are not powered, ice or thermo containers are required. In fact, this is the norm for smaller events. Finally, when there is no electrical supply, the cooks should be prepared to serve the dishes without the use of slicers, blenders, mixers, and other small equipment.

Traditionally, catering companies bring all meals to a catering destination at a high level of readiness, minimizing the need for reheating, plating, and decorating. Tableware is brought in quantities sufficient to avoid washing dishes during an event. For banquets, the plate and silverware count is assessed based on the number of planned meal courses, with a minimal fallback margin of 10–15 percent.

Catering a buffet is more complicated because it is difficult to estimate how many times the guests would need new plates, stemware, or silverware. The minimal estimate is three units of tableware per guest for a very short event up to three hours long. The maximum estimate is five units per person. This is typically sufficient even for a very long event. It applies to the most common tableware: a snack plate, fork, and a nonalcoholic beverage glass (highball). Knives are typically used less and can even be eliminated altogether depending on the menu. Cups for hot beverages should be estimated according to the count of ordered tea and coffee. The same goes for glasses for alcoholic beverages. It is safe to assume that no more than four or five glasses of any kind would be used by any guest.

It is important to discuss the other elements of table decoration. Before the guests taste any food, their first impression is based on the decor of the dining hall. And the first impression, naturally, is priceless. Decor elements may include wrought dish racks and glass-and-mirror support plates that can also work as serving dishes for desserts. The same glass-and-mirror surfaces can serve as support for flower bouquets. Various fabrics are essential for draping the tables. Five to ten years ago, table skirts were a standard for most formal events. Today there is a trend toward plain fabric and simplicity. Of course, the key element of decor is the tableware itself.

If desired, some dynamism can be added to an event by way of various culinary demonstrations. This calls for specialized equipment.

A carving station can be used at a catered event to serve meat and fish. Decorative carving of fruits and vegetables remains relatively uncommon.

Champagne or chocolate fountains remain guest favorites, although to professional caterers, this may seem like an outdated concept.

A crepe station with a crème maker and multiple filling containers will most certainly attract guests.

A good find is an "egg animation" station equipped with a tiny stove with a built-in gas balloon and a boiling-water vessel. The cook cuts off the top of a raw egg in a shell, discards the egg white, and puts an eggshell with the egg yolk into the boiling water. After a few minutes, the egg is served with grated parmesan, caviar, or any other ingredients on an egg stand.

At times, it is possible to add excitement with the most trivial equipment. A few years ago some catering companies tried a service called "buffet lady" where the guests are greeted with drinks and hors d'oeuvres by a waitress or a fashion model. She is placed in the middle of a round table on wheels, and her dress is a stylized continuation of the tablecloth. There are drinks and hors d'oeuvres on the table, and the waitress can move around among the guests. This is typically used to welcome guests to an event.

All in all, catering companies must look for inventive ideas everywhere and anywhere, because our customers expect and highly value our ability to surprise and impress their guests!

PART 7

Formats of Off-Premises Catering Events

Various Types of Catered Events

There is an endless variety of classifications for catering service formats. In order to discuss the nuances of different formats, we will also have to agree on some basic classification.

The following is a very typical scenario. A potential customer tells a customer service manager, "I would like to order a buffet catering service for our event."

An experienced manager replies, "By buffet service, do you mean that guests are not seated at tables and freely walk around the venue and socialize? And food and drinks are served on buffet stands and bars?"

The customer response is "Of course not! Everybody must be served at tables."

Sometimes customers mention some strange service format like banquet-buffet or banquet-cocktail. Why is the word "banquet" a necessary component of all these formats of service? Anyway, so as not to be confused, let's introduce some common terms.

A banquet will mean the format where all guests are seated at tables (everybody has a seat). What's most important is that the guests are served by waiters.

The next format is the buffet. This will mean dishes are served along buffet stands. There are variations regarding menu content, the way dishes and drinks are served, and, finally, how guests are placed. The buffet menu can consist only of refreshments—something that can be eaten without a knife, only with help of fork, or without any cutlery at all (so-called finger food). Or, in contrast, a menu can include various dishes of a wide assortment and formats of plating and serving (salads, hot and cold refreshments, main and side dishes, and desserts). Drinks service will be located in separately organized bars.

In a buffet setting, there are traditional variants regarding guest placement. Guests may be seated at tables. Here the only difference from a banquet is that guests come to buffet stands for food and to bars to get a drink. Waiters collect dirty dishes. However, buffets can do without guest seating, which allows guests to walk around freely. Sometimes a compromise of the two is with organized, partial guest seating. In the case of partial or complete absence of seating, provide high cocktail tables so that guests can comfortably socialize and enjoy food and drinks while standing.

An even livelier and more dynamic format of service is a cocktail party. Furniture can be absent entirely (but not necessarily). In this case, food and drinks are served on trays and served out to guests by waiters. This format imposes strict limitations on the prepared menu. Only compact finger food refreshments that can be eaten without cutlery are relevant. A typical solution is canapés or bowl foods. Certainly, cocktail tables can also be used in this format. Drinks are usually served in bars to simplify the process.

We should also speak about barbeques as a separate format. Here hot dishes are cooked in the presence of guests on open flame.

The format of the menu and the format of service are not the same thing. You can serve a cocktail menu on buffet stands, and banquet dishes are often served in a buffet format.

You shouldn't strictly adhere to one format of service in all situations. It's quite acceptable to have a fusion of formats. The main principle you should be guided by is to choose the optimal format for the customer.

For example, waiters deliver drinks (often only champagne, wine, or soft drinks) and light refreshments to an audience who's waiting for the rest of the guests. So it's evidently a cocktail format. But when all guests gather together, they will be invited to the main hall for a gala dinner in traditional banquet format with full seating. Hence, two formats work side by side at one event, although they separately adhere to their patterns. Another example would be that all the guests sit at their tables, where they are served with several courses during the evening. However, desserts and hot drinks are served on buffet stands.

A customer, in fact, isn't concerned much about what format is chosen. As a rule, the customer is more worried about comfort of his or her guests than about strictly observing canons of a format.

What Determines the Choice of Format for an Event?

When choosing an event format, we should consider some essential factors, including aims and purpose of the event, number of invitees, length of service, any limitations caused by the chosen banqueting space, and also allocated budget.

Let's take an event for five thousand guests at a stadium as an example. The banquet is for the best sales reps of one big retail company. Three hundred fifty of the best directors will be invited to the stage for diplomas and awards, so everybody will be called by name in turn. Apparently, this event is going to be a long one. Hence it's better to choose a format with seating for service. Moreover, taking into consideration the number of guests, the most comfortable variant is a banquet.

If time allocated for an event is very limited, it's better to forget about the banquet format. For example, for an event lasting less than one hour, it's more reasonable to choose the cocktail format or a buffet as a last resort. If it's a New Year's company party lasting five or six hours, it definitely requires a banquet format or a buffet with full seating.

Chosen space can also impose some limitations on the event format. First, consider the open-space banqueting area. In small spaces, you'll have to make a choice in favor of a buffet with partial seating or without it instead of a banquet. The second limitation, which we can't ignore, is the shape of the chosen banqueting space. A hall with plenty of architectural details like columns, balconies, and multilevel staircases would be very inconvenient for a banquet format. In this type of venue, a buffet without any kind of guest seating seems a good solution. The requirements and limitations that the administration of a banqueting hall imposes also play an important role in choosing the format. For example, a countryside mansion prohibited use of any porcelain or glass dishes at events for fear that glass breakage could threaten visitors of this mansion-museum the next day. It's easy to imagine that it's impossible to organize a banquet with such limitations (using only plastic dishware).

When financial budgets are limited, it should be evident that we offer a modest cocktail party when something more serious like a banquet seems unrealistic.

Space and Shape of a Banqueting Hall for Organizing Catering

We should outline some basic rules; breaking them will definitely create some problems.

The first rule can be considered a general truth of catering business. Food and drinks must be placed in proximity to each other. For example, when servicing an event in a spacious banqueting hall, it's not recommended to serve food and drinks in distant parts of it. It would be a mistake, if servicing an event on a double-decker ferry, to place buffet counters on one deck and place a bar on another. We should view the last example in greater detail.

Buffet stands, bars, and tea stations are often placed on a lower deck that is not exposed to weather conditions. However, in fine weather, guests spend most of their time on open-air upper deck. Consequently, there is a desire to change the organization of service to accommodate guests. As we have already mentioned, it's impossible to "split" food and drinks. We can just place an extra bar on the upper deck. And exactly here, as a rule, the main mistake is made by shifting to the cocktail format of service. In this case, the level of service will suffer in all areas. The truth is that the staff at the event are in charge of the following areas of work: maintenance of buffet stands in working condition, serving the bar, and collecting dirty dishware. As soon as we try to involve the staff in serving guests with food and drinks on trays, we will certainly make them pay less attention to preexisting areas of responsibility.

Let's view a specific case. Let's say there are fifty people to be served on a ferry. We need one or two waiters to maintain a small buffet counter, one to be responsible for a bar and one or two waiters for collecting dirty dishes. So when we shift the staff from these main responsibilities to guest service, we involve one waiter from a buffet counter and one waiter from collecting dirty dishes. Therefore, guests will be served by two waiters. But the waiters are unlikely to cope well with such a task, given the fact that utility space on ferries is traditionally located on the lower deck. Therefore, the waiters will have to move around the whole double-decker ferry. At the same time, other components of the service-buffet line and used-dish collection will lack attention. A bartender removed to the upper deck will either leave the lower deck without drinks or pour them out for free access and leave the guests of the lower deck without service at the bar station.

The second catering rule deals with adequate estimation of the number of bar stations, necessary for serving guests with drinks in buffet format. First, bars should be equally distributed throughout the event space. At the same time, it wouldn't be a right decision to put the only bar station in the middle of the banqueting hall (this would be relevant only in a club format, where getting a drink in a bar as itself is a self-sufficient component of a party). It's important to provide even distribution of bar stations all over the event space for the guests' convenience. You can base your estimation on the fact that one bar is optimal for serving fifty guests, if we mean individual servings of every portion of a drink. Or up to one hundred guests served, if a bartender only needs to pour out drinks into glasses that guests take from a counter themselves. In case of serving large-scale events, we can join bars putting two or three bartenders at every bar station, making them larger.

The third rule allows you to avoid so-called "dead areas." An uneven concentration of guests in different parts of a hall is a fairly common effect of inconveniently shaped event space. To make the most of all of the space, you should invigorate the areas that tend to be "dead" by placing certain elements there. For example, you can place a chill-out area in such places. If a format of an event allows, it's better to give a potentially "dead" area for DJ work and a dance floor if possible. One may also place tea stations and buffet counters with desserts, if they are not served in the main area, as a good solution. If cocktail tables lack in the main area, they can also be a good element to "revive" dead areas. That said, don't duplicate what is in the main event area. To be more exact, do not place additional buffet stands and bars because they are unlikely to attract guests' attention, as guests are more willing to put up with the inconvenience of cramped conditions in the main area of the event than to be out of center of action.

The fourth rule consists in keeping the minimal distance between the hall where guests are served and the utility space where dishes are plated, dirty dishware is collected, and kitchen utensils and dishes are stored. The farther away a utility space is, the longer waiters will be absent from carrying away dirty dishware or serving. This will immediately impact the level of service and be noticed by the guests.

The fifth rule concerns the care of organized dirty dish collection. Otherwise, it would quickly remind you of itself. Dirty dishes tend to accumulate in places where they are very undesirable. It's necessary to put some tray jacks (big trays on pull-down stands) or small draped tables along the perimeter of the hall where the event takes place to avoid this problem. It's important to observe certain conditions for greater functionality. Do not place any chairs or seating places next to them, or they immediately turn into a guest seating area. You also mustn't put some ashtrays on them, which would make them a smoking area and a guest concentration place that would hinder service. The only thing that can be placed on them is napkins. If a place is organized in the right way (we'll talk about it a bit later), all the guests of an event are able to perceive the function of these places and use them accordingly. Certainly it's important to have people in charge of these dirty-dish stations, otherwise it wouldn't make any sense to put them there.

Dirty-dish collection is an especially burning issue for events where guests get access to buffet counters only for a limited time—for example, during a lunch break at a conference or a buffet during a performance intermission. All guests leave a lot of dirty dishes in a short period of time, and catering service is sometimes unprepared for this situation.

The Size of a Hall Necessary for Different Formats of Service

Minimal space per person necessary for organizing service in a banquet format is 16.2 square feet (1.5 square meters). This number should be considered the lowest. If space is below this limit, it's better to refuse the banquet format and choose another variant. If we have more space than stated in the limit, it would only add comfort to placing guests. Increasing banqueting space up to 3, or even more square meters for a guest will not create any negative moments.

The aforementioned limit includes space for placing chairs, tables, and necessary aisles. So for a banquet seating of one hundred people, you will at least require 1,620 square feet (150 square meters), which will be enough only for chairs, tables, and small aisles. The rest of the space necessary for organizing the event, like space for placing a stage, a dance floor, guest meeting areas, and so on, you should count additionally.

For convenient organization of banqueting space, you can create a schematic table arrangement on a scale, where tables are depicted as circles in the diameters of the real sizes of tables and chairs, and aisles are taken into account. For example, using a table with a diameter of 5.94 feet (1.8 meters), allocating some space for chairs and aisles around it, 20 and 10 inches (50 and 25 centimeters) respectively, we get a total diameter of 10.89 feet (5.94 + 1.65 + 1.65 + 0.825 + 0.825), which is 3.35 meters. It's not difficult to operate circles when planning banqueting space on a scale, because they already include size and dimensions of the table as well as space for chairs and aisles. You can place circles on a schematic—elbow to elbow—due to the fact that aisles are already taken into account. We allocated for aisles only 0.825 feet (25 centimeters) from each side of a table; that means that the aisle between two nearby tables is 20 inches (50 centimeters). Of course, that's not much space and acceptable only in situations when we try to define minimal space. If we have more banqueting space, we can leave more distance between tables, which would make guests feel more comfortable.

The minimal space for servicing guests in buffet format is 10.75 square feet (1 square meter) per person. This space is enough for servicing a buffet without guest seating. It includes space for placing guests, buffet stands, bars, tea stations, tables for dirty dishes, and cocktail tables, if planned. We welcome more space, if it's possible.

If we are planning a buffet format with full guest seating, it will require even more space than a banquet format, as we need space for placing buffet stands, bars, and tea stations. Generally speaking, it will take a bit more than 17.5 square feet (1.6 square meters) per person. For servicing guests in buffet format with partial seating, the minimal amount of allocated space will depend on what proportion of guests are seated. There are no limits or standards regarding the amount of guests seated; the key factor here is the space of a hall chosen for an event. In addition to tables where guests are seated, there should be some cocktail tables where guests can socialize while standing. Such an approach to buffet organization entails that guests mix during the event and there is no assigned seating.

Finally, cocktail service requires the least space. We can talk about slightly less space than is required for servicing a buffet without guest seating. This would be about 8.5–10.5 square feet (0.8–1 square meter) per person.

Preparations before an Event and Time Requirements

A big amount of work is done on the day of the event before it starts: unloading and setting up furniture and equipment, arranging dish delivery from a warehouse, unloading, setting up the banqueting space, arranging tables and chairs and their coverings and decorations, polishing dishes and cutlery, and arranging dish presentation and table settings. At least three hours should be allotted for all these operations, even for small events. Of course, experienced employees can prepare within one hour in case of pressing need. But is this extreme worth it? Moreover, such things as employee briefings, changing uniforms, and mealtimes for staff should also be included in the above-mentioned list. It's also useful to have a backlog of time in case of emergency.

For global events, furniture, equipment, and other necessary things are often delivered on the eve; only dishes are delivered directly on the day of the event, and waiters start draping and setting tables in the morning, eight to ten hours before guests arrive. Sometimes, part of the work is done at night before an event—for example, chair and table draping and polishing silverware and dishes.

"Behind the Curtains"

In the catering industry, every event happens at a new venue. This means that off-premises catering has to organize its work differently for every location. A stationary restaurant needs to fine-tune its work only on its own premises. This includes "behind the curtain" work in a utility space, which is hidden from guests' eyes. In catering, utility space is new every time. So in the preparation stage, we have to work out some guidelines for organizing this space and implement it to work literally in one day. Due to this fact, we need to clearly understand the sequence of loading a truck or van before delivering all the necessary equipment to the venue. Items necessary for the most time-consuming work must be available first for unloading. These areas are arranging and draping the furniture and dish plating by cooks (of course, if dishes are delivered not plated in Gastronorm containers, which is widely practiced). So furniture, textiles, Gastronorm containers with food, and kitchen utensils must be unloaded first. After that, you can unload glasses, drinks, and expendable materials.

It's essential to provide control of equipment flows during unloading. Often unloading doesn't happen directly into the provided utility space. It's usually done in several stages—let's say, from the truck to a service elevator and from the elevator to the necessary floor and then to the utility space. In reality, this transport can be difficult, and its every step must be controlled to avoid equipment loss because of negligence and/or employee inattentiveness.

At the first stage of equipment unloading, control can be exercised by a driver. A technical manager arrives at the event for the next stage of the unloading. The manager then forwards the equipment with help of porters or waiters to the utility space. If a catering company works without technical managers, this function is then delegated to a banquet manager (event manager). Presence of a manager in the utility space is especially important at the unloading stage: all the work of servicing the event greatly depends on how this space is organized. In the utility space, a manager organizes equipment distribution, stockpiling similar positions and making them conveniently accessible.

However, despite the importance of a manager's presence in the utility space during unloading, the manager can't ignore all the intermediate stages. For this reason, the presence of one more manager (technical manager) during unloading is quite sensible. In the case when a manager has to work alone, he or she must actively move along the unloading pathway and be "everywhere at the same time." Certainly, the manager can appoint employees to be in charge at every stage to optimize control. But it would be more of a compromise, and failures could be avoided only at small-scale events.

If a catering company always involves only one catering manager for the whole event and doesn't see any sense in involving others, we can assume that its management has no idea of how many problems and failures happen in reality. By the way, in the premium market where service requirements are especially high, a position of installation manager is introduced for loading in a warehouse, transporting, and unloading at a venue.

When organizing a small event, a manager can easily cope with the optimal distribution of functional areas and equipment in utility space. If a global event is being planned, it's better to prepare a detailed organization plan of the utility space illustrating all functional areas. For example, you need to place several tons of equipment in a space of 5,000–10,000 square feet (450–1,000 square meters). This means that it will be impossible to change something during preparation to the event or its servicing. Therefore, any mistake in the organization of the utility space can cause big inconveniences in work and as a result influence the level of service.

Space and Requirements for the Utility Room

Minimal space for the utility area per guest is 2.2 square feet (0.2 square meters). This space is approximately the same for any format of service. More space will only add comfort. Consequently, utility space of at least 220 square feet (20 square meters) is required for servicing one hundred people, and 2,200 square feet for servicing one thousand guests. If the utility space lacks square meters, you will have to work "in the field," temporarily replacing utensils and equipment in nearby territory, under stairs, in corridors, and so on. You cannot do with less space during an off-premises catering event.

It's worth mentioning that if a catering company works without plating dishes at a venue and brings them fully plated on wagons, it will require slightly less utility space, due to the fact that they allocate little or no space for cook's prep. For work at a rented venue or on a customer's premises, its administration will require you to provide lists of employees, delivered equipment, and vehicles and also solve the problem of protection of flooring against involuntary damage. Considering the fact that caterers are never provided with a professional kitchen, its substitute usually is a room without fade-resistant carpet flooring, expensive parquet, or custom-designed tiles. A catering company often has to bring a roll of thick polyfilm to cover the floor to avoid arguments over damage compensations.

Often, there are questions about running water, electrical consumption, and canalization (for pouring out drinks leftovers). All of these require timely coordination in the framework of general technical preparation. In regard to garbage removal, we can view several variants. Small amounts of garbage after a smaller event can be removed by a company's own forces. But considerable amounts of garbage require significant time and workforce and sometimes even an extra van or truck. So it's better to order a special garbage-removal service. Expenses for this service at global events will be much lower than payment of employees' extra hours (plus spent time and organization and control of this process).

Tents, Umbrellas, and Other Outdoor Equipment

Off-premises caterers often have to rent tents for outdoor work, which ensures independence from weather conditions. Some companies have their own tents, but that's more an exception then the rule. Professional tent construction requires quality maintenance, storage, forwarding, installation and dismantling. Catering companies try to avoid this, preferring rental companies working in this field do their job.

Tents often become a significant expense in the estimate of costs for an event, and a customer usually tries to optimize expences, reducing the space of rented tents. However, you should take into consideration the weather peculiarities of a region. Let's say, in sunny Spain or Cyprus where it hardly ever rains in the summer, you can organize service without tents without any apprehension. However, in London or New York City, it wouldn't be a well-considered decision. If a company had sold off-premises catering services on some date and at some time, and it started raining exactly on the event's day, the company wouldn't be able to fulfill contractual obligations. Bad weather wouldn't be considered a *force majeure*. Caterers can't prevent customers from cutting budget on tents for placing guests outdoors, but tents for utility space and tables should be a must-have for making outdoor catering possible in any weather.

Companies offering tent rentals are ready to provide extra services and equipment—in particular, heaters (gas forced-air heaters, fan heaters, lantern heaters), hot-air curtains, climate-control systems, electricity generators, partition walls, folding screens, fences, textile draperies, and modules of wooden floorings. If there isn't any solid asphalt, concrete, or wooden surface under the tents, modules of wooden flooring will be necessary for using banquet furniture. Otherwise, the legs of the banquet chairs would drown in the earth, and only light plastic chairs would be available for use.

Shapes of Tables for Servicing Different Event Formats

Different-shaped tables can be used in organizing banquets. For example, one common table or separate tables, which are more widely spread. A common table is used for private events or chamber events with relatively small numbers of guests. For the majority of company events, it's better to give preference to separate tables of different shapes: round, square, and rectangular. The round table is classic for the banquet format. Typically, round tables have a diameter of 4.95 or 5.94 feet. Rectangular and square tables are more rarely used and can be different sizes. For a buffet service, table linens can be one- or two-sided in a shape of lines, waves, or rings or in combinations of different forms. A buffet line becomes one-sided when it's located along the wall; sometimes little space is left between the wall and the tables to make it conveniently accessible for waiters but not too wide to enable guests' access. If you locate a table line in the middle of event space, it will be double-sided and accessible for guests from both sides. In the absence of organized guest seating, you'll need high cocktail tables 3 feet 37 inches (1 meter) high with a diameter of 24–32 inches (60–80 centimeters) in addition to table lines.

In a buffet format, with organized guest seating, it's necessary to combine table lines and separate tables of any shape for guest seating. It would be impractical to use only one common table in this situation. Tables for off-premises catering must be either portable or pull down for easy transport.

Necessary Size of Tables and Staff Standards for Service

To service one guest in a banquet format, 24 inches (60 centimeters) of table perimeter is standard. For a table with a diameter of 4.95 feet (1.5 meters), we find that it's acceptable to seat eight. A table with diameter of 5.94 feet (1.8 meters) allows us to seat ten people. In reality, ten people are often seated at a 4.95-foot table and twelve at a 5.94-foot table. Such an approach is not acceptable for all events. We can consider 20 inches (50 centimeters) as minimal space. Guests sitting at a round table feel less discomfort compared to those sitting at rectangular ones of the same "length" because round tables give the effect of mutual remoteness. Often, limited banqueting space leads to the necessity to minimize the number of tables and compromise with more cramped guest seating. Sometimes the number of tables is decreased for cost cutting, including rent and drapery cost.

One waiter is able to serve one table where eight, ten, or twelve guests are seated. If there are VIPs at the table, the number of waiters is increased. It can be one extra assistant for every two tables or a second waiter per table; sometimes individual waiters are assigned to certain guests.

Nowadays, there are two widespread variants of banqueting service: silver service and plated service. In the silver service, all courses are served by the waiters from large serving dishes with serving tongs or cutlery. Portions of the courses are placed onto guests' plates. Plated service is considered a higher style of service and means that waiters serve plated dishes individually to each guest.

An especially high style of plated service is called a simultaneous drop, when dishes are concurrently served to all guests. In this case, we need one waiter for every two guests. If guests sit at one long rectangular table, two lines of waiters come to the table from different sides and stand behind the guests. The first waiters in the lines are supervisors; they exchange nods to make the process simultaneous. Every waiter has two portions of the next course. The first waiter puts a dish in front of the first guest, the second in front of the third, and the third in front of the fifth, and so on. All waiters perform concurrently with their supervisor. After that, rising straight, waiters put the plate from the left hand to the right. Supervisors again exchange nods, and all waiters make a step right to the next guest. Also simultaneously, the line is guided by the supervisor's actions. If the supervisor is difficult to see, the waiters look to the waiter closest to the supervisor. Again simultaneously, waiters put the dishes on the table in front of every guest. After that, they stand erect and hold for a second. Then, in beautiful synchronicity, they leave the hall. Guests often applaud.

When guests sit at round tables—for example, for ten people—and it's not possible to involve a large number of waiters, simultaneous serving is still quite realistic if five waiters from nearby tables join in one team and serve table by table.

A la carte service is hardly ever practiced in catering with the exception of working with VIPs. There are two variants of a la carte service in catering. The first is "staging," which is a restaurant form of service. This involves taking the order and serving the chosen dishes. All dishes are already cooked and delivered to a venue. The second option is a real order with fast cooking of the ordered dishes from partially ready ingredients. In practice, a la carte service is rarely done.

In the buffet format, ten guests per 3.3 lineal feet (1 meter) is an established standard. Consequently, for organizing quality service for fifty guests, you will have to set a 16.5-foot table (5 meters). If you organize a double-sided buffet counter and provide access from both sides (by putting the counter in the center of the hall), it will work more efficiently. In other words, you'll need a 33-foot line (10 meters) of counters for servicing one hundred people if you place counters by the wall, but you can do with a 16.5-foot (5 meters) double-sided buffet counter (without decreasing the amount of food).

With the buffet format, there are lots of nuances in spatial organization. For example, hot drinks can be served on counters in open-access areas or in the bars. With open access, some employees will maintain these tea stations in working condition with the collection of dirty dishes and by bringing the necessary amount of teacups and saucers, renewing napkin holders, and so on. If cocktail tables are used, they should be assigned to certain employees. Smoking areas must be separate from the main event space, and somebody must work there too. Therefore, the total amount of staff can vary greatly in a buffet format.

However, we can and must estimate an amount of involved staff. A conventional number of bartenders is one for fifty to one hundred guests, depending on the service format. The number of waiters is estimated as two for every 16.5-foot (5-meter) length of buffet counter. For servicing cocktail tables and tables where guests are seated, one waiter is necessary for three to five tables in buffet format. In the case of partial seating, you'll have to place stations for the collection of dirty dishes and cutlery and for employees to serve them. Certainly the collection of dishes by waiters "on the fly" seems a great alternative, but it hardly ever happens in practice. Each job involves considerably more human resources, and they become a significant part of the estimate of costs. A buffet with a difficult organization of service requires the same number of waiters as banquet service: one waiter for ten to fifteen guests. With a very simple buffet, this number can decrease.

PART 8

The Menu for Festive Occasions

Appetizers, Hot Meals, and Desserts—How to Account for Everything

A traditional catering menu for a banquet or a buffet includes salads, cold and hot appetizers, main dishes with sides, and desserts.

Today, healthy eating is important to most. So the ubiquitous mayo and heavy, multicomponent salads are out of favor. In many instances, customers request hors d'oeuvres instead of salads. However, salads are still popular for variety, albeit in smaller volumes. Sometimes they are even placed after cold appetizers in the menu, not before as they used to be. Shared salad plates are still practiced, although the search for new ideas for salads does not cease.

Hors d'oeuvres are often served in tart shells, now that heavy tartlets made of thick dough are a thing of the past. Often salads are served as bowl food, in martini glasses or whiskey tumblers. Something like a French salad made of pear and cheese cubes in yogurt can be even served on a lettuce leaf, and a colorful mix of fresh vegetables can be placed in bright-yellow bowls made of cheese. China spoons, frequently used in Japanese cuisine, turn out to be an interesting miniature salad plate also.

So what types of dishes and what quantity should be included in a menu? On one hand, it depends on the format of the event; on the other, it depends on the extravagance desired. As discussed, the most common forms of catering are the buffet, banquet, and cocktail reception. Each scenario involves a certain range of dishes depending on the cost and level of service. Cocktail receptions will be discussed separately.

A buffet table can include three to five salads. In a banquet menu, one or two options will suffice. In this case, it is either possible to serve one plated salad to all guests or offer a choice between two options, if the service supports it. There is also a more exotic option of serving both salads on one plate to each guest, although it is crucial to remember that it positively won't do to combine salads that don't go well together (such as a fish salad and a meat salad).

A buffet line should include eight to twelve cold appetizers. At a banquet, when appetizers are served plated, the range can vary from one appetizer, a choice between two appetizers, or a selection of hors d'oeuvres offered on one plate. In many countries, it is becoming popular to serve shared appetizer dishes on the table. In this case, it is recommended to offer an assortment of five to eight appetizers.

With regard to hot appetizers, it is uncommon to offer more than one or two. They are either presented to the guest to choose or served in turns, as long as they go well together. At a buffet line, hot appetizers are offered on chafing dishes, similar to main dishes.

There are various approaches to a buffet menu. Some consider it appropriate to only serve hors d'oeuvres that can be eaten with a fork and without a knife. Others don't hesitate to include traditional dishes with sides that guests can eat at a cocktail table or even seated.

In a buffet line, there should be from two, as a minimum, to four hot meals. It is unlikely to have more than that. The hot meals are placed on chafing dishes. At a banquet, it is often sufficient to offer just one hot meal. Less often, a catering company would offer a choice of two or three options. In this case, sides are typically assigned to each specific option. In some cases, two main dishes are served to each guest in turn, but this is an exception rather than the rule.

Desserts at a buffet can be offered in a broad assortment. As with other courses, the rule is that variety can only do a buffet good. It is quite reasonable to include a minimum of three to five types of desserts. At a banquet, it is typical to serve only one dessert to all guests or offer a choice between two options. Another appropriate choice is an assortment of miniature pastries on a plate.

When fruits are chosen for service, they deserve individual attention. While fruit is always a nice addition to any menu, simply serving cut fruits is bad form. In the premium market, it is common to include miniature exotic fruits and berries in the menu. In the medium and in the economy markets, it remains a tricky question as to how to serve standard items such as apples, pears, etc., when only a few have been ordered. When it is not possible to offer whole fruits and cutting is unavoidable, we can recommend a few options. For example, fruits can be served as a brochette (with small pieces on a pick) or a salad in a dessert bowl. Both are well received by guests.

With regard to a cocktail reception, all dishes in the menu would be either sweet or savory and should be served as a canapé or bowl food. Simply speaking, it gives you four types of hors d'oeuvres. In each type, anything goes, as long as the assortment in each group is alike. Since the reception format is commonly at events of shorter duration, the assortment rarely exceeds twelve to fifteen dishes.

Seasonal Specifics of Meal Selection and Catering

There are certain peculiarities in selecting and plating dishes in summer and winter. Of course, it is especially important in regions with distinct seasons. In winter, heavier, denser dishes are more popular, with sauces that are served even with appetizers. Products that are generally considered "risky," such as potato salad, rice, liver, and so on, are used more often. Certain banquet dishes such as sturgeon or roast pig are especially popular in winter. In the summer, guests prefer light dishes with simple recipes and fresh ingredients that haven't been thermally processed. If the main dishes in the menu are grilled, portions should be more significant, because barbecue and kebabs often become the centerpiece of the event!

However, in any season the assortment should be diverse, and the yield should not vary significantly. Depending on the region, different seasons might impose different transportation requirements. For example, it would be difficult to transport dishes in hot summer without isothermal equipment.

Menu Volume and Yield

Apart from the overall importance of menu assortment and variety, it is crucial to consider the necessary yield. The menu volume would vary significantly in different countries.

At an event of three to four hours long, in any catering format, in Western Europe or North America, it would be considered normal to yield six hundred to eight hundred grams per guest. At the same time, in Eastern Europe or Russia, the standard yield would exceed one kilogram. These numbers are average per person, whether a strong man or a delicate lady on a strict diet. This yield is not a required minimum; it includes a certain margin, since buffet lines should not be completely emptied by the end of an event. Besides, guests' appetites are unpredictable.

Naturally, the main part of the menu will be consumed in the first half of an event. After that, the guests' activity declines. Slightly reducing or increasing the duration of an event would not significantly affect the yield. It is important to note that the yield does not account for canapés when guests arrive or for beverages.

When catering a buffet for more than two hours, it is not recommended to place more than half of the meals on the line at the beginning. The rest should be supplied by waiters as and when necessary during the event. Otherwise, the line gets emptied right from the beginning, which produces an unpleasant aesthetic impression.

Main dishes should not weigh less than 250 grams, including sides, although making them heavier than 400 grams is impractical. In summer, grilled dishes can weight 300–350 grams per guest without sides; 250 grams without sides should be considered an absolute minimum.

When a celebratory cake is offered in addition to other desserts on the menu, it should yield 70–100 grams per person as a minimum.

How to Produce an Attractive Menu within a Given Budget

It is a common misconception that reducing the assortment while keeping a standard yield results in significant savings. In reality, there would hardly be any economic benefit, even with the most compact menu. The load on the cooks is only slightly reduced. Maintaining the same yield requires almost equal labor efforts. Certain savings are possible when complex, multi-ingredient dishes are replaced with simpler ones and when expensive and exotic ingredients are excluded.

The total cost of catering is optimized only when all expenses are impacted. Therefore, the menu should only be changed when the catering format, staff count, and transportation methods are all optimized. For example, for one buffet event of one hundred guests, one truck may be sufficient to transport all meals and equipment. However, catering to the same number of guests at a sit-down banquet would require a second truck just to transport chairs. Therefore, even with the same menu, transportation expenses would be twice as much because of the change in the catering format.

The yield of a buffet menu can be reduced if an event is very short; four hundred to five hundred grams per guest can realistically suffice. As far as a cocktail reception goes, with miniature hors d'oeuvres served on picks, just ten pieces (canapé or bowl food) per guest may do. With an average piece weight of twenty to thirty grams, the entire yield will be approximately two hundred to three hundred grams per person. However, if a reception will be long, and it is desired to really nourish the guests, twenty to twenty-five pieces per person, at the total yield of six hundred grams, may be necessary.

After approving the menu and yield of each dish per person, a customer often asks: How can I control the vendor? How can I weigh the catered dishes? Is it possible, if at all? The answer is really simple: yes, it is possible, when desired. If a customer attempts it without warning the caterer, it can be quite unconstructive and will constitute complete lack of trust between the customer and the vendor. It means that the catering managers lacked the professionalism to convince the customer of the reliability and integrity of the catering company at the time of booking the service and event preparation. It is also an odd behavior for a customer to mistrust the vendor while not refusing the service altogether. It is not a common sight to see a customer representative at a catered event methodically weighing dishes on a scale, but it does happen!

Beverages–Necessary Yield and Assortment

The yield of refreshment beverages at an event three to five hours long, not counting tea, coffee, or alcohol, is 1–1.2 liters per guest. It can be less for shorter events and more for longer events of six to eight hours.

At high-end events, the assortment of beverages typically includes only juices and water, while in the middle and economy segments, they can also include soda such as cola or tonic. Depending on how many categories of drinks are provided, the yield can be divided in equal parts: for example, out of the total of 1.2 liters per guest, 400 milliliters in juice, same in water, and same in soda. In its turn, the total yield of water can be divided in equal parts between still and carbonated water, and the same with different types of soda. However, juices are different. Typically, at least one-half of the entire yield of juices should be orange juice, as it is the most popular. The rest can be divided equally among other juices.

For example, one-third of the 1.2-liter yield, in juice, would be divided into 200 milliliters of orange juice and 50 milliliters each of other types: apple, tomato, and juices such as pineapple, cherry, grape, cranberry, or grapefruit. This approach to supplying the beverage bar typically eliminates any problems. An exception should be made for events with a very small number of guests. For example, at an event of only twenty guests, it is reasonable to only plan 1 liter of tomato juice (i.e., just five glasses). But if the event is three hours long, it would be entirely possible that tomato juice would be most popular. Therefore, at smaller events, it is recommended to increase the yield of each type of juice, mainly by way of reducing the assortment. At larger events, juice consumption levels out, and the problem eliminates itself.

Hot beverages can be offered in various forms: as leaf tea and freshly brewed coffee at a high-end event or bagged tea and coffee in the economy segment. It is worth mentioning that bagged doesn't always equal cheap or low quality. There are many very decent brands on the market. Brewing espresso coffee and tea can be done with the help of coffee machines. Teapots are only used in the premium segment, and even then not often. However, it is not recommended to serve ready-made tea or coffee in a thermo container, unless it is brewed right on the spot. Office-type water coolers and dispensers are not practical for catering because they are not designed to provide streaming hot water.

Whichever type of tea or coffee is selected by the customer, it is recommended to prepare with a 20 percent reserve (e.g., 120 cups per hundred guests). In a buffet, the tea station should be prepared before the event begins, although the beverage itself should not be served before dessert. Otherwise, in order to offer tea during the entire event, a much higher yield is required. For a banquet, it is wise to get the customer's approval to serve hot beverages, not uniformly at a set time but as requested by individual guests. This way, the workload will be better distributed between the servers.

There are several aspects to take into consideration with regard to serving alcoholic beverages. When expensive champagne is served, guests tend to consume it frequently and with great pleasure. However, a simple sparkling wine would only be consumed for a cause, such as when toasting with guests at arrival, at the management speech, for New Year's or wedding cheers, and so on. When no toasts are planned, the yield of only 0.15–0.2 liter of champagne per person is reasonable. With regard to wine, the yield can vary in the range of one-third to two-thirds of a bottle (1.5 to 3 glasses per guest) depending on the following two factors: the duration of the event and the assortment of hard liquor in the bar. The longer the duration and the shorter the assortment, the higher the yield.

Beer is not always suitable at catered events, and even at a summer beer reception it is unlikely that guests would drink more than three units per person, be it a pint, bottle, or can (0.33–0.5 liter). Besides, those who drink more would be offset by those who don't drink beer at all.

A nice addition to the catered assortment of alcoholic beverages would be cocktails. Naturally, not every customer would request them. But when a catering company includes them in the commercial offer, it should decide in advance how to prepare and serve them. Mixing cocktails at the kitchen facility would be wrong, and preparing them immediately at the event should be planned so that the company can satisfy the requested number of glasses. The issue is that when cocktail ingredients are visible in a bar, any "connoisseur" can demand from the bartender to mix grenadine with tomato juice or Cointreau with tonic. As a result, it would be impossible to produce the promised 225 glasses of a specifically ordered cocktail. To avoid this issue, cocktails should be mixed at the utility area, inaccessible to the guests, or at a separate cocktail station that does not mix any other drinks.

Corkage Fees

Also known as a bar tax or cork tax, the corkage fee has nothing to do with the taxation system. It is the industry slang for charging a customer a fee for bringing his or her own alcoholic beverages. In most restaurants, only beverages bought inside may be consumed. However, that is difficult to enforce at a catered event, since it might be taking place in someone's country house or in an office. In either case, a customer may disagree to only use beverages supplied by a caterer.

To serve beverages, the caterer would still need to supply glass (and therefore transportation, loading and unloading, dishwashing, and other services), a bartender, ice cubes, and so on. To compensate for such expenses, it is typical to charge a corkage fee. Sometimes, when a customer pays to serve his or her own beverages, the caterer can additionally agree to load, transport, and unload the bottles and then return unopened beverages from the event area to the customer. Some caterers do not charge the corking fee at all, while others, as a rule, offer various discounts to incentivize particularly attractive customers.

The Dishware Count

Catering can be done in places that lack water, sewage, and electricity. It practically exists as an answer to the demand for a restaurant service in a place that is not equipped for it. Among other specifics of catering, it is notable that tableware is not washed at an event space. It is brought in a quantity, sufficient to cater without washing dishes, and transported back unwashed.

Where a stationary restaurant typically stocks up all types of tableware in a quantity of two units per dining place, catering requires much more. At a banquet, it is easy to calculate a precise count of tableware based on the number of meal courses. A minimal reserve of 10–15 percent is added to the base. Only textile napkins are used, although in the economy segment it is fine to offer napkin holders with paper napkins on the tables in addition to textile napkins. That practice is unacceptable in the middle segment and, of course, at high-end events.

Catering at a buffet is more complicated. Besides plates, there are forks and knives as well as highball glasses for nonalcoholic beverages. When only hors d'oeuvres are served, it is possible to get away with no silverware at all. In all other cases, forks and knives are required (the latter is used much less but is considered a necessary part of the serving etiquette). All popular positions should be planned for at a count of three to six units per guest. We discuss this in more detail in the chapter 22 dedicated to catering equipment.

Glass–To Have or Not to Have?

To reduce the cost of catering, sometimes plastic tableware is used. The savings are generated by way of lower cost of transportation, loading and unloading, and washing and polishing glass and in less breakage. Of course, plastic is only appropriate in certain situations. It can't be used at a banquet event. However, it might be appropriate at an informal open-air picnic in an economy segment. The yield of disposable tableware is about ten units of each type per guest, mostly plastic glasses, plates, and cutlery.

Besides the savings, choosing plastic tableware can be justified by matters of safety—for example, when catering to an open-air corporate event with alcoholic beverages at a beach.

The Menu Price

What to include in the menu price and what to charge separately depends significantly on the market. In certain regions, it is customary to include delivery and service in the menu price, therefore eliminating the need to further negotiate with a customer. In highly competitive markets, it is typical to discuss every expense in great detail. At times, the customer would even want to discuss the cost of renting tables for the cooks in the utility area. In the markets where caterers rent tableware, it also becomes a separate line of the budget. Vendors that own tableware can specify that the cost is included in the menu price. The cost of transportation, even when included in the price, only covers city limits. Any trip to the countryside should be discussed separately.

The menu should always show the yield of each dish. It is convenient for customers when the yield is per person. Otherwise, anecdotal situations are possible. For example, when a stationary restaurant got into catering, the personnel continued to apply the old rules to the new business. The yield of a Caesar salad is 200 grams, and Greek salad is 250 grams. The manager decided that two salads with a total yield of 450 grams per person would be too much. Therefore, applying the stationary restaurant mentality, he decided to include fifty portions of Caesar salad and forty portions of Greek for one hundred guests. Presumably, 10 kilograms of each salad would yield 100 grams of salad per guest. However, when a customer sees an offer that lists fifty portions of Caesar plus forty portions of Greek salad for one hundred guests, the customer is left puzzled. The customer would be similarly surprised to see 110 portions per one hundred guests. The manager is used to making kitchen orders as a count of portions from the menu. But in catering, the counting should be done in a way that is meaningful to the customer, not to the catering team. In practice, it is the best to show the yield in grams or ounces per meal per person. Therefore, the menu should include not a count of portions but the yield in grams or ounces per guest, especially since the price is given per guest. This way, the customer can immediately assess what he or she gets for the budget. And as far as a kitchen order goes, a manager can rewrite it in any form that is customary internally.

Sometimes the menu price includes additional items such as nonalcoholic beverages. They are inexpensive, and the assortment is standardized. Certainly, a customer may request specific beverages, but it is rather an exception. Sometimes the menu also includes tea and coffee. This is undesirable in the economy and middle-market segments. Including cheap bagged tea and coffee signals to potential customers that a caterer works in the economy segment, which would contradict the image of a high-end caterer.

In the premium segment, a menu can include hot brewed beverages, but in most cases it is wise to put them as a separate line of expenses and present a customer with several options. The same is true with alcohol. A menu for a New Year's banquet can include a glass of wine or a well-known brand of champagne, but in most cases alcoholic beverages should be negotiated separately.

Canapés and welcome beverages can either be included in a menu or offered separately as a "welcoming reception menu." In this case, to avoid a prolonged negotiation, it is not advisable to list the entire assortment of canapés. It is better to offer a tried-and-true package that includes various canapé items that go well with wine and champagne. The count of canapés and beverages would depend on the duration of the welcoming reception. Typically, three canapé varieties, one glass of wine or champagne, and one glass of nonalcoholic beverage per guest are sufficient.

Traditionally, the cost of catered dishes and beverages is slightly lower than meals in a stationary restaurant of a corresponding quality. One of the main principles of catering is a lower profit margin per portion with higher sales volumes. Second, restaurants have the ongoing expense of rent, which is included in the price of the meals. When catering requires renting an event space, the cost is a separate budget line that is discussed with a customer. Third, restaurants serve to the final consumer: a person who orders a meal and pays for it. In other words, restaurants sell dishes to single guests per plate. Catering sells meals wholesale. In one evening you can serve a number of guests that many restaurants won't even be able to fit, and they would have probably had to close their space for a private event. A catered event by definition adds dozens, hundreds, or even thousands of dining places to the existing space.

Caterers often stipulate a minimal order. It is quite justified, because any catering company can assess the minimal budget that would be profitable.

For example, one company could cater up to twelve events a day. It had a truly impressive annual volume of events. At the same time, it did not have a minimal order. A simple analysis showed that 35 percent of the events it catered to only brought 5 percent of the revenues. The Pareto rule states that 80 percent of a desired result almost always can be achieved using only 20 percent of the resources. In that company's case, there was a clear evidence of unproductive efforts. To cut off those 35 percent of events that hardly generated any profit, it was necessary to introduce a minimal order of merely $600. After that, the company not only retained 5 percent revenues but even experienced growth because its managers were now able to redirect their efforts from unprofitable orders to the key customers. Of course, there are always exceptional situations to consider, and any catering company can find itself serving small events for VIPs and loyal customers.

Calculating the Menu Price

The price of a dish in a menu of a stationary restaurant is typically calculated using the following formula:

The price = the food cost x markup

Let's review it in detail. The food cost of a dish in a restaurant is the only variable cost. When there are no guests, there are no food costs. Lots of guests mean high food costs. All other expenses, including rent, utilities, and salaries and such, are fixed costs. The markup in the formula compensates for the fixed costs and generates the desired level of profit.

There are situations when a restaurant wants to calculate a total price of a catering menu that would include the cost of transportation and service that can be presented to a customer as a price per guest. What happens to the formula? The restaurant incurs expenses that were previously unaccounted, such as engaging hourly waiters and cooks, which becomes necessary as soon as the original headcount is not enough. Add the cost of transportation that a stationary restaurant did not have at all. The formula transforms into the following:

The price = the food cost x markup + hourly personnel + transportation + miscellaneous

What is wrong with this formula? The issue is that transportation and hourly personnel in catering are variable costs. How do we separate the variable costs that should be covered with markup from the ones removed? There is no simple answer. Most professional catering services that offer their customers a menu price per guest use a different formula:

The price = (the food cost + hourly personnel + transportation + miscellaneous) x markup

Of course, the value of markup in this formula is different from the one used in a stationary restaurant, since the base cost is considerably higher and includes larger variable expenses. The resulting price can stay the same.

For example, one company applied a markup of 500 percent in its stationary restaurants, but in the catering service it used 400 percent in the original formula, as the profit margin in catering may appear lower than in stationary dining, but the sales volumes are higher. When the company switched to a catering formula of the menu price, the multiplier matching the same price was only two, so the markup was only 100 percent.

The larger the city where a catering company operates, the higher the demand and, therefore, the higher the markup.

PART 9

Methods of Organizing Hourly Personnel for Catered Events–Adhering to Corporate Standards

Specifics of Work with Hourly Personnel

Significant seasonal fluctuation in demand is very typical for the catering industry. There is also no consistency in the scale of events that a particular company caters. Catering companies work with events of varying scale. Of course, each company has a certain capacity limit, but most strive to continuously grow and expand. Some even say that there is no limit to a guest count that they are prepared to cater to. This creates certain conditions for working with personnel.

Staffing needs in catering vary considerably from event to event and from one month to another. For example, an event of twenty guests requires, theoretically, a couple of servers. When catering to two thousand guests, two hundred servers may be needed. In December, a catering company may need a large headcount, but in November it would need much less. Therefore, it is impossible to determine a practical permanent headcount of waiters because from time to time they will be either insufficient or idle. The same is true with other personnel roles.

Traditionally, catering companies attract temporary employees. Freelance and hourly personnel include cooks and dishwashers (kitchen workers), servers, and bartenders, as well as truck loaders. It is important to note that most catering companies also employ a number of permanent cooks that supervise hourly personnel and essentially perform the duties of sous chefs. Naturally, no two companies are alike. For example, in some companies, waiters perform the loading duties, while in others serving and loading is split between two different staff roles. In some countries, there are also companies that hire exclusively male servers, although in the United States and some other countries, this would be an illegal, discriminatory practice.

In order to supply sufficient personnel for any event, catering companies either form their own databases of hourly personnel or work with staffing agencies that specialize in temporary personnel. In many cities, the average age for a waiter is nineteen to twenty-five, and most are students or unskilled workers. The level of accountability of such personnel is pretty low. As a result, there is a certain statistical rate of absenteeism among hourly workers. In large cities, this rate can amount to 10–15 percent. Certainly it can be reduced based on how thoroughly a company maintains its staff database, but it is practically impossible to achieve a 100 percent presence rate. It is therefore important to account for possible absenteeism and engage more personnel than strictly needed.

In smaller cities, the absenteeism rate can be significantly lower due to a different demand for waiters. The smaller the city, the less the demand, and as a result, there are fewer alternative opportunities for waiters. By contrast, the bigger the city, the larger the catering market. When catering companies compete for personnel, workers are less loyal because they always have other opportunities at their disposal. Of course, even in a large city it is possible that all hired waiters will show up to work. Then the caterer can either decide to dismiss a few, offering them a certain compensation for the false call (e.g., a fee for a couple of work hours) or retain all waiters for a number of hours before dismissing a few and paying them for the actual work. Either way, the benefit is in the ability to choose whom to keep and whom to dismiss.

Besides the absenteeism, it is important to know how many workers from a database can be reliably contacted in time. For example, a catering company with a database of four hundred waiters may be able to have at an event about one-fifth, or eighty workers. This is an average that varies between companies and depends on the size of a city. The smaller the city, the larger the number of workers that can be reliably reached. In order to contact as many freelance waiters as possible for a large-scale event, it is advisable to start making calls a week or two before the event. It is different with cooks, though, because they are typically more mature and inclined toward stability. With a database of fifty cooks, it is realistic to get response from up to thirty or even more.

Different catering companies have different opinions with regard to the required level of qualifications for kitchen workers. Some tend to hire highly skilled workers and pay them handsomely, while others attract workers with basic skills and rely on permanent cooks to supervise them.

We should mention that most companies keep serving and truck loading duties separate, as they understand that waiters involved in loading equipment at the kitchen will not have time to shower and freshen to provide excellent service at the event. It is still typical to require loading duties of the waiters at smaller events. When surveying freelance waiters, we note that there is a category of freelancers who consciously choose to work only with the companies that do not make them load trucks. By separating these two functions, a company increases its potential to broaden the waiter database.

As far as truck loaders go, the peculiarity is that they are needed only for a few hours before and after an event, which is challenging for both the caterer and the workers. Sometimes this issue is mitigated by way of employing the loaders as stewards who perform various casual duties such as packing dirty dishes during the event.

As mentioned before, catering companies also use agencies that specialize in temporary hires. Their services cost 1.5–2 times the salary of a waiter a company can attract from its own database. But without a doubt, it is easier than developing your own contact base. These agencies can often source not only the operating personnel but also supervisors and forepersons. These workers with managerial functions can be a huge help to a catering manager in charge of an event. Agencies source several types of waiters. The first type is only good to pick up dirty dishes. The second and more advanced type has certain experience at various catered events. And the third type is highly experienced. The hourly rates can be two to three times different. Naturally, any catering company is interested in forming its own contact base with a purpose of ensuring stability and a higher measure of control. But agencies can be excellent partners in preparing and catering to a large event.

In large cities, it became the norm to pay temporary personnel by the hour. In contrast, in smaller cities it is common to pay a fixed fee per event. Since the catering service was born in large cities that have a longer history of catering, it is easy to imagine that eventually hourly pay will become the convenient norm.

Working with a Personnel Database

Let's highlight that the quality of work in any company, be it catering or otherwise, should be based on workforce management, not personal traits of individual employees. So when working with temporary personnel, it is important not only to develop a large contact base but also to apply a systematic approach to managing the workers and enforcing corporate standards of work.

When recruiting temporary workers, forward-thinking catering companies ask the candidates to fill in a detailed questionnaire and provide a photo and a copy of an ID. Selected data from the questionnaire is then entered in a database so that it is possible to look up the information about any worker. Usually the database includes the name, uniform size, height, phone number, and e-mail address of a worker. It may be useful to include the address, since the personnel are often needed at odd hours when public transportation is not available. For countryside events, it may become handy to know whether a worker has a car.

On a separate note, it is very important for any caterer to form an idea of what a worker is like. For that, it makes sense to add to the database a "category" field. It doesn't have to include many options and can be limited to basic descriptions of "excellent," "average," or "bad." It can also mention if a worker has senior and/or managerial experience and can potentially supervise others. This information should only be included after a worker has taken part in at least one event. An event manager should update the information in the database based on the experience. In the future, this information can be edited if a waiter gets better or worse. When choosing servers for an event, "excellent" workers are approached first, and others are approached only when necessary. When there are not enough of the "excellent" and "average" workers and the "bad" ones are to be brought in, it does not necessarily mean that the caterer is willing to compromise on the service. The better the worker, the less supervision is required. And by contrast, the worse the worker, the more managerial supervision is needed.

The database should also contain information about absenteeism. When a server commits to an event but does not show up, he or she is marked in the database, say, with a mark of "1." If the server was absent for a second time, he or she is marked with a "2." In this case, the server should be deleted from the database.

Anyone who notoriously violates the rules of conduct in a particular catering company should also be eliminated. Most common violations in catering include theft, consuming alcohol on duty, nibbling food in the presence of guests, and/or inappropriate behavior with the guests. Over time, more and more companies prohibit smoking while on duty. Workers that are eliminated for violations should be included in a blacklist to prevent their reappearance in the database. Any company that denies having a blacklist is either deceiving or lacks necessary quality controls. For many years, catering companies in one city exchanged their temporary personnel blacklists so that a waiter who broke the rules in one company would not find employment with others. Of course, that was a rare situation. The exchange was mostly used as a motivating factor to incentivize the waiters to be exemplary. Similarly motivating is when companies prioritize hiring "excellent" workers. Blacklists and worker categorization are sometimes mentioned when a catering company instructs workers before an event.

Companies that are new to the catering business often attract waiters among the students of hospitality schools. Companies with a few years of experience expand their databases by way of their waiters bringing in "friends and acquaintances." So over time, the situation changes, and instead of the company looking for waiters, waiters start approaching the company, and the issue of candidate search eliminates itself. To cater to particularly large events, all caterers work with agencies that specialize in temporary hires.

Systematic Approach to Workforce Management

To ensure efficient workforce management, it is important to standardize certain business processes. For example, it is necessary to have a standard procedure of entering a new hire in the freelancer database. During the first interview with a server, two parts are necessary: collecting certain information from the candidate and communicating key information to him or her. At the first interview, the important aspects of work should be communicated to the candidate, including the pay rate and schedule, existing rules of conduct (for example, no smoking during an entire event), possible fines, and so on. Entering a freelancer's data into the database should be standardized so that all necessary information is collected and all necessary work conditions are communicated to the candidate. Further, there should be a standard procedure for calling staffers to work. This would include the information about the date, time, and location where a server should show up, how much he or she will be paid, what duties are expected, what time he or she can expect to be finished, what he or she should bring to work, and what rules and limitations will be in effect. A manager that calls temporary workers should be careful to deliver all this information. The worker should also be informed how and whom he or she should notify, in a timely manner, if the worker cannot attend. We describe the procedure of entering new hires in the database, as well as the procedure of calling a waiter for work, in the chapter 9.

In order to be able to consistently provide the highest quality of service to the customers, every catering company should develop its own standard procedures for its daily internal operations as well as business processes that directly relate to catering, serving event tables, waiter conduct, and so on.

Multilayered Management System

Since freelancers are involved irregularly, based on a catering schedule, it is unwise to expect that they would learn the rules of conduct by heart and, further, that they would remember them. Furthermore, many hourly waiters work with multiple catering companies, each with their own standard procedures. As a matter of fact, temporary personnel cannot be reliably trained to enforce corporate standards over a long time. Only permanent employees, in particular the event managers, can be trusted to carry out the corporate standards.

The only way to compensate for the lack of preparation and training of the waiters is by way of efficient supervision by staff managers. In this light, it is very important to consider the so-called "span of control," or the maximum headcount that one manager can efficiently supervise. In the managerial science, the optimal number is believed to be seven plus or minus two—in other words, a range of five to nine workers. The exact number depends on the complexity of the work, workers' professionalism, and so on. Skilled workers conducting uncomplicated activities can be supervised in large numbers. However, when dealing with highly technical work, a manager should limit the number of subordinates. The same applies when the work involves elite responsibilities or calls for higher qualifications. Waiters are considered to be operational personnel with a limited range of responsibilities, conducting uncomplicated work in terms of required competencies and skills.

It is no secret that most events require more than nine waiters. What should you do, when it is impossible to adhere to the span of control—when there are too many waiters for one event manager? In this case, managerial science suggests a measure of so-called intermediary management. In plain language, waiters are divided into manageable groups that are supervised by a foreperson or a senior waiter who serves as an intermediary between the waiters and the event manager. The manager doesn't have to supervise all the waiters—only the intermediaries. For example, for twenty to thirty waiters, two supervisors would be practical. Each would oversee ten to fifteen workers and report to the manager. This is called a multilayered freelance management system. This system can include managers, supervisors, and assistants. Of course, it is mostly practiced by companies who prioritize top-level service and are willing to pay the price to maintain it. Most companies in the economy segment could not bear the additional expense of hiring managerial employees for a catered event and, therefore, control and the highest service are not always present. By far, not all companies, even in the middle segment, practice this approach.

Let's review an example. In a large banquet hall with an area of 12,000 square meters (130,000 square feet) is a relatively small space for an event of 650 guests. A reception area is planned to greet the guests and a banquet area for the gala dinner with sixty-five tables of ten diners. The tables will be placed around a dancing floor (the event is a ball) in three circles. The first, with twenty tables, is intended for VIP guests. Each of the sixty-five tables will be served by one waiter and, in addition, there will be ten assistants at the VIP tables, one assistant per two tables. In total, we will need seventy-five waiters in the banquet area. In the welcoming area, we plan to utilize some of the banquet waiters, who will later shift with the guests to the banquet area. Additionally, we will keep five waiters stationary in the welcoming area. Besides, in the utility room we will have a group of cooks supervised by a chef. There will be a technical manager with a couple of assistants who will supervise the movement of the equipment. All in all, the event manager will supervise eighty-four workers, not counting the cooks. It is obvious that if the manager is left to supervise this headcount alone, there will be no semblance of order at the event, and the manager might not even learn about all the issues that will transpire. Therefore, intermediary management is necessary. A dedicated supervisor—ideally, a second manager—should be assigned to the welcoming area. The second manager will report to the event manager.

Realistically, the welcoming reception will be an event of its own, a short buffet-style event for the 650 guests. As stated, in the banquet area, the tables will be placed around the dance floor in three arches, essentially forming three sectors, each including the first, second, and third row from the dance floor. Each sector should be assigned a dedicated supervisor with an assistant. In summary, for every twenty-five waiters in each sector, there will be two supervisors. Overall, in the banquet area, we will have three supervisors and three assistants who will manage seventy-five waiters.

Beyond the banquet territory that will be cut out of the total area of 12,000 square meters (130,000 square feet), there is a "blind" zone that is not controlled by the manager and supervisors. That creates a risk of undesirable events. Waiters can sneak out to that space to skip work and so on. Some would say that it never happens, that the personnel are reliable and can be trusted. While we certainly wish that to be true, in reality the true question is what we can see and what happens beyond our knowledge. Ideally, we should place an assistant in this blind zone to remind the waiters about the rules of conduct, track the time they spend visiting restrooms, and so on. It is also wise to ensure that waiters do not spend excessive time in the utility room.

It is possible to assign freelancers, especially those who have grown in the waiters' ranks, to a supervisory role. However, the assistants, due to the nature of their duties, should be picked exclusively from the ranks of permanent employees. The reason is that assistants often have to implement unpopular, harsh measures against the waiters, and they should remain absolutely impartial and objective. Supervisors and assistants should stand out among the waiters by way of a different uniform or a formal office dress.

To sum up, we have an event manager who supervises a team of ten people: a welcome area supervisor, three supervisors in the banquet area and their three assistants, an assistant in the blind zone, a technical manager, and a senior cook. To complement this multilayered management system in the conditions of a particularly large space, key personnel should be supplied with walkie-talkies. For example, the main course has been planned to be served at 8:30 p.m., but the customer is asking to delay it by fifteen minutes. The event manager uses the walkie-talkie to inform the senior cook and all supervisors. Without the walkie-talkie, the event manager would have to run around the hall, missing other important matters. Besides, at high-end events, the guests can approach the waiters with various exotic requests: someone asks for cigar cutters, another inquires about a blanket, and the third refuses any food except steamed vegetables. The waiters are not always equipped to answer such requests and at best will consult with a supervisor. If it is beyond his or her authority, the supervisor can contact the event manager on walkie-talkie, and the manager in turn can consult with the customer. As a result, the situation remains under control, and the guests receive prompt answers to any questions. Of course, at most basic events such a level of attention would be excessive, and it remains the question of the level of service that a particular catering company would like to provide.

In present day, this example of workforce management would be quite rare. For most managers, having a team of supervisors and assistants at their disposal would be a remote dream. The issue, though, is not the workload imposed on a manager but the manager's capacity to perform his or her duties, what happens without his or her knowledge, and how this impacts the quality of service provided by a caterer. And the latter, unfortunately, often leaves room for improvement.

Besides the matters covered above, for efficient workforce management it is important to plan workforce flow during an event. For the best control, it is desirable that waiters move between the catering hall and the utility room on one single path. It is also important to plan the workers' flow within the catered area and within the utility space, to keep it simple and unified.

It is crucial that freelancers be informed in detail about each stage of their work. I suggest conducting three phases of training. In the first phase, the team is divided into working groups, each with its individual supervisor. The initial training should be conducted as early as possible, as soon as the personnel arrive. Before the personnel are assigned individual supervisors, they all report to one manager. If the team is large, workforce management is inefficient. Until the personnel are informed about the rules of conduct, they operate without rules and is essentially unmanageable.

During the initial training, waiters are instructed with regard to basic rules of conduct and their duties in preparation for the event. It is too early at this stage to discuss the procedures of guest service since people will promptly forget.

The second phase of training is conducted at the end of preparations and before the guests' arrival. At this point, the basic rules are reiterated, and the outline of the event is discussed: what dishes and beverages will be served when and what to keep in mind while serving. After that, individual training is conducted within each group by its supervisor, directly at the work area. Again, the rules of conduct are repeated, and then each worker is instructed with regard to his or her duties. The manager and supervisors should prepare the instructions in writing. All three phases of a template training procedure are described in the chapter 9 that talks about documentation of catering processes.

Providing Meal Service for the Workforce

It is important to plan how to provide food for the workforce. At smaller events that last 1.5–2 hours, it will be unnecessary to provide meals for workers. But at any lengthy events, it might be required to feed the workers not only during the preparation phase but sometimes even during the event itself.

For example, when catering to a countryside event of a large scale, a company had to set up the equipment the day before, and on the day of the event, the waiters had to start at ten in the morning. After having their breakfast at home, the waiters arrived to work. Before the event began at six in the evening, they were served lunch. The event lasted till midnight. After that, time was spent cleaning the area and preparing for loading the trucks—duties where the waiters were also actively involved. As a result, most did not leave till 2:00 a.m., and one meal since 10:00 a.m. was insufficient.

Some catering companies try to walk away from offering their workers any meals, asking the waiters to bring sandwiches and lunch boxes from home. Most companies do prepare special meals for the workers. Either way, arrangements must be made for the workers to enjoy their meals in an organized fashion. Otherwise, expecting them to "find what and when to eat on their own" can result in undesirable situations that would primarily harm the caterer. Instead of providing quality service to the guests, the waiters will be concerned about finding food.

Efficient and practical arrangements include a few simple elements. First of all, one of the cooks at the event should be additionally tasked with supervising the meal service for the workers: handing over lunch boxes, bread, water, and disposable tableware. Second, a meal area should be assigned, away from the routes that the waiters take during the event. For example, it can be located in a far corner of the utility room. This way, even if the personnel in the utility room can observe the waiters eating, they would be prevented from joining in. The reason is that while it might be possible to feed the entire team simultaneously before the event begins, during the catering the waiters would not be allowed to leave the catering hall in large groups. In reality, the meal area is often placed at the entrance to the utility room, and as a result any waiter who enters the space might be tempted to join those who were specifically relieved by the manager to take a break. It causes unplanned shortages of waiters in the catering hall and unnecessary time and efforts by manager to find them and return them to work.

Third, it is important to carefully plan the meal breaks. It should be a relatively long stretch of time when there is a minimal load on the waiters—for example, the interval between serving the main course and dessert. And fourth, it is necessary to determine how many waiters should take a break simultaneously. For that, count the logical sectors of an event space, and determine how many waiters can be absent from each sector without impacting the quality of service. After deciding on the count of waiters, establish how many break sessions will correspond. For example, if out of thirty waiters only six can be absent at a time (two from each of three sectors of the catering hall), then in total it will take five meal sessions. Knowing that the total interval of available time is 1.5 hours, we establish that each group of six will have about eighteen minutes (local labor laws will need to be adhered to regarding meal breaks as well). Senior waiters and supervisors will have to diligently control waiters' breaks to adhere to the allocated time. Until the first group is back to work, the second group cannot leave for its break. These simple rules allow you to efficiently plan meal breaks and ensure that waiters are fed in an orderly fashion.

A separate, lockable room should be provided. Waiters should change in the mandatory presence of a company representative. If at a later time someone needs to get back in the room (for example, to retrieve something he or she forgot), the representative must accompany the person in the room, observe his or her actions at all times, and lock the room afterward. When no changing room is available, the waiters can leave their belongings in a cloakroom, if it is present. Otherwise, in field conditions, they leave their clothes with the technical manager, and nobody can access them without his or her permission. This way, catering companies minimize theft, among other issues.

There is a limited arsenal of incentives that a catering company can use in application to temporary personnel. It includes categorizing the workers in a database with an aim to prioritize "excellent" workers and blacklist violators. This should be conveyed to the waiters during their initial training. Additionally, it is recommended to offer two pay schedules, one for novices and one for experienced waiters.

Each catering company would only value the experience a waiter gained on its own events, because each company has its own standards and specifics. When talking about monetary incentives, the following is important. Some think that supervisors should be paid extra for their additional responsibilities. However, it proves to be inefficient, because when supervisors compare the insignificant difference in pay rates with the significant increase in responsibilities, many decide that they are quite content to remain ordinary waiters and not be accountable for others. It is much better to offer a lump-sum bonus based on the results. While the final amount might not be different from an increased pay rate for supervisors, psychologically it works better. Also, unexpected, *force majeure* increases in workload should result in additional compensation. For example, when twelve waiters are called for a high-season event where only ten are required, but less than ten actually show up, they should receive a bonus for working extra—from the original budget that was planned for ten people.

PART 10

Specifics of Preparing and Catering for Large-Scale Events

What Is a Large-Scale Event?

A large-scale event is always a challenge for any company that works in the field of customer service, including catering. When I say "scale," I do not mean a guest count exceeding a certain specified number. For a catering company that normally serves events with 20 to 50 guests, an event with 150 guests would be large scale. At the same time, for a company that regularly caters to events with 1,500 guests, large scale would mean 2,500–3,000 people or more. Scale varies per company. Certain companies that are in the small, boutique events provide a very high level of service. Catering to a large number of guests is only impressive when it is performed confidently, relying on service technologies that produce consistent, unyielding quality. By far, not all players in the catering industry can claim that they have a systematic approach and possess all the desired tools of managing service operations.

The first element that is absolutely necessary in catering to large-scale events is a proper preparation plan. In case of smaller events, the plan can be in a manager's head, especially when these small events take place several times a week. However, when dealing with an unusual scale of event, the manager will quickly find that his or her existing skills might not be sufficient. Besides, large-scale events include so many elements that managing them "on the go" won't work.

Preparation Schedule

A written schedule of preparation, written in advance, helps the manager to exercise control and have a clear understanding of what time is at his or her disposal and whether he or she is on track to complete all the necessary activities with an average speed or should switch to urgent mode.

The schedule is written in a table format that includes three key indicators: the time, the responsible party, and the activity.

When marking the time frame for various activities, it is the best to use half-hour intervals. On one hand, half an hour is a lot of time. On the other hand, it is short enough to keep the duration of tasks reasonable and easy to control. Half-hour intervals should not contain any contingencies—they should be reserved for the end of preparation. The contingency will come handy in case of any *force majeure*. Normal activities should be performed at a brisk pace. Do not create an environment for the personnel to relax and take advantage of the contingency buffer.

Divide the waiters into convenient, manageable groups, following the span-of-control formula. Assign them to senior waiters (forepersons or supervisors). This should be done right after the equipment is delivered to an event space, as soon as the personnel arrives; otherwise, an event manager would have to deal with an uncontrollable crowd for a while. Thus, his or her control over the workflow will be an illusion.

When filling out the activities field, consider that duties should be divided between the catering hall and the utility area. Also, activities are divided into types: main and support tasks (including training, personnel meal breaks, and dressing) and consecutive or recurrent tasks (for example, steaming chair slipcovers), which are performed throughout the entire preparation time in conjunction with other activities.

Let's review a template preparation schedule for an event of seven hundred guests. The event will be served by twenty waiters and twenty waitresses divided into two groups of mixed gender of twenty servers each. Each group is assigned one supervisor who directly reports to the event manager. During the preparation time, the manager only communicates with the supervisor, tracking the fulfillment of the schedule and providing instructions. Supervisors make sure that the personnel meet these deadlines. The personnel do not have the entire schedule—there is no need to provide them with the information beyond their duties. If a manager would like to change plan for the next half-hour interval, he or she can arrange the schedule as needed without wasting time in conversation with all supervisors.

The beauty of following a schedule is that the manager doesn't have to worry about deadlines and doesn't have to keep them all in his or her head. The manager just sets objectives for the supervisors and checks with them twenty to twenty-five minutes later. Was the task done successfully, or was a deadline missed? The manager can then decide what other intervals to use to compensate for the delay.

A manager without a schedule can succeed, and the event would probably still start on time. But it will cause the manager much more stress and is much less efficient.

The Documentation Package

The schedule is a tool to organize the work in a calm and efficient manner, but it is only one of many documents that a manager needs while catering to a large-scale event.

The manager should write down all the information that he or she accumulates as a project administrator, in order to later send it to relevant departments of the company to keep them in the loop. Otherwise, the manager will have to manage all processes alone. If he or she doesn't prepare a furniture layout in advance, at the event he or she is responsible for it. No description of table setup? The manager will have to prepare the first table. The list of rented equipment is absent? The manager will have to personally receive the delivery. When all these documents are prepared in advance, he or she can delegate the table setup to supervisors and waiters and the equipment receiving to the technical manager.

So for an event of "ordinary" scale, a manager can successfully do with a small list of documents. These are the necessities: the equipment list, textile list, beverage list, transport schedule, customer menu, functional list (all additional information about the event), personnel list with the arrival time and location, and written instructions for the staff.

For a large-scale event, the list is much longer. The following are added to the previous list: preparation schedule (as described above) and furniture layout across all areas with the electric power supply points marked and the entry points for beverages and dishware. Then, of course, there is a graphic scheme of the table setup, complete with a textual description and a general scheme of meal courses that outlines their quantity, types of serving dishes, and the time of serving. Important note—the scheme of the meal should be supplied to the executive chef so that he or she will know when to have appetizers, main dishes, and desserts ready, and on which plates and in what quantity.

Additionally, it is crucial to have a diagram of the utility area. When there is only one small truck with equipment, it is possible to first set up the utility room in one way and then move it elsewhere. But at a banquet the size of a stadium, there will be no time, hands, or energy to move everything around. It should be installed once and for all.

Ideally, all blocks—hot beverage station, cook station, equipment storage, dirty-dishes table—should be equidistant from the entrance, so that waiters can easily reach each place. When that setup is not possible, try to place the kitchen and the dirty-dishes area closer to the entrance. Hot beverages will only be needed once during an event, and the equipment storage can also be pushed away.

Certainly, try to place the utility area close to the catering hall. The shorter the walk for a waiter, the faster the service. Ideally, the utility area should have a separate exit that will allow the removal of dirty dishes during the event, out of the guests' sight.

The documentation package that a manager prepares for a large-scale event should include a file with all the customer correspondence—a document that shows what was discussed and what questions were brought up. Additionally, include a copy of the customer agreement, the rental agreement for the catered space, the event script, records of equipment handed over to the waiters, and template forms for extending an event. I always recommend including in the agreement that an event can be extended per the customer's request, with each additional hour costing 2–5 percent of the original cost. To record the fact of extension, the template form is filled in with the requested time and immediately signed by a representative of the customer.

In summation, the manager ends up with a hefty folder. The day before the event (typically for large-scale events that is when the equipment is delivered), the manager gathers the technical manager, the executive chef, and the supervisors and hands them the copies of documents that pertain to their duties.

Don't attempt to compile a file in one or two days. It is impossible. It usually takes a week, during which time the documents are frequently amended and expanded. This is due to the fact that customers tend to make changes until the last moment. When an event is over, you will have precious records. If it is a recurring event, next year you will be glad to have this archive because nobody can remember all the tiny details. It will also be useful when working with the same customer at a different space or for a different type of event.

For new managers who have less than two years of experience, I would recommend accumulating the records even for smaller events, such as three hundred guests.

Smoking

In the early 1990s, most catering companies didn't mind their waiters smoking. Toward the end of the decade, the first "villains" emerged who said no to cigarettes. Today, a total ban is the norm. And it is not only because of the smell but because of the lack of control. When smoking breaks are permitted, we equate a habit to a physical need, which is very individual. You encourage one, even three breaks in a shift. A server can say he or she needs to smoke every fifteen minutes—that's the server's physical need. What would you say? I have heard of companies that try to track it and introduce break passes. When you are managing many dozens, sometimes even hundreds of waiters at a really large event, imagine that they start taking smoking breaks, and when you need them, you can't find them.

Imagine a "director banquet" of five thousand guests from a large cosmetics company, taking place in a large stadium. Four catering companies, each with its own sector and utility space, serve it simultaneously. Waiters from a company that is lax about smoking (and generally is not strict about controls) sometimes end up on the other end of the stadium! Obviously, in this situation only a few waiters from the entire headcount would really care about providing quality service.

Working Two Shifts

Catering companies frequently find themselves contemplating whether they should hire two shifts of waiters for an event that takes a day or more between preparation and catering. The benefit of changing horses in midstream (and waiters in the middle of a banquet) is arguable. But every country has labor regulations that have to be complied with. Is it possible to perform for twenty hours while constantly standing and smiling?

Once I served as a manager at two events of a particular catering company. During the first event, an open-air space was divided into two areas with 250 guests. Staff managers served as supervisors. I asked them to stay in the catering zone with the waiters throughout the entire time. They were not used to it; usually they have an opportunity to step away, sit down, and take a break when there is less fervor. Later they told me, naturally, that it was an impossible task. Virtually two days later, I was at another event, a banquet with 320 guests, where supervisors were appointed from the ranks of experienced waiters. They were new to this function. They performed the role without any issues and were quite happy with the bonus added to the regular rate. So a twenty-hour shift is not that scary. In the end, there is such a thing as working one day on, three days off.

The Space

Planning the space for large-scale events is also a critical issue, where the aforementioned challenges become particularly vital. It is important to eliminate any "dead spaces" by placing there activities not available elsewhere. Examples could be the dance floor, a tea or coffee station, and so on. Also, I recommend observation over blind areas and carefully planning the workforce traffic routes.

In summary, a large-scale event is always a trial of a catering company's capabilities. But it is not as difficult as you would imagine. It is much more difficult to build a working system of processes that will allow you to work confidently with any serious, large-scale events—not with one's last strength but in a routine and calm manner.

Conclusion

Catering service is both complicated and exciting. And like any other business, it is full of subtleties and details. It is only possible to be successful in this industry, as in any other, when you love what you are doing and when you strive to do your best in anything you undertake.

The catering market is dynamically growing, offering multiple opportunities for evolution of the catering service itself, individual catering companies, and the industry in its entirety. There are companies that owe their existence to the fact that their owners were not satisfied with a subpar standard in existing service and decided to strive to change for better.

It is should be known that in the long term, only quality products and services are competitive. When you are in a position to offer the market a quality service, it is important to differentiate yourself from others and make the distinction glaring.

I would like to wish all who already work in catering or are just considering it to adopt the best practices developed in this industry over many years. There is no need to reinvent the wheel. Also strive to help this service evolve further by practicing it every day in a high-quality, professional, creative, exciting, and enthusiastic fashion!

I will sincerely enjoy reading your feedback and questions with regard to the matters described in this book or any other issues that arise in your personal experience. Send your letters to cyrillpogodin@gmail.com.

About the Author

Cyrill Pogodin

Mr. Pogodin began his career in catering in 1997 while simultaneously obtaining a master's degree in business administration. For ten years, he was the hands-on managing partner of Cascade Catering until it was sold in 2007. He catered large-scale events for as many as twenty-five hundred attendees at more than seven hundred events. The list includes AIG Life, American Express, Avon, BIC, Boeing, Bristol-Myers Squibb, BP, Cable & Wireless, Cadbury, Caterpillar, Coca-Cola, Colgate-Palmolive, Deutsche Bank, Ford Motor Company, Gillette International, Heidelberg, Hewlett Packard, HSBC Bank, IBM, Johnson & Johnson, Kimberly-Clark, L'Oreal, Mary Kay, McDonald's, Morgan Stanley, Moulinex, Oriflame, Philip Morris, Philips, Renault, SAP, Schneider Electric, Schwarzkopf & Henkel, Skanska, Sony, Stimorol, Sun Chemical, Tchibo, Thomson, Unilever, Volkswagen, Volvo, White & Case, York, and many others.

Mr. Pogodin is now an internationally known and respected catering consultant and has taught seminars and visited over one hundred catering companies in such countries as Australia, Belarus, Finland, France, Germany, Great Britain, Italy, Japan, Kazakhstan, Russia, Spain, Sweden, Ukraine, and the United States.

Made in the USA
Lexington, KY
15 December 2017